Also by Alain de Botton

On Love
The Romantic Movement
Kiss & Tell
How Proust Can Change Your Life
The Consolations of Philosophy

.

The Art of Travel

ALAIN DE BOTTON

PANTHEON BOOKS

NEW YORK

All rights reserved under International and
Pan-American Copyright Conventions. Published
in the United States by Pantheon Books, a division
of Random House, Inc., New York. Originally
published in Great Britain by Hamish Hamilton,
an imprint of the Penguin Group, London.

Pantheon Books and colophon are registered
trademarks of Random House, Inc.

A Cataloging-in-Publication record has been
established for *The Art of Travel* by the Library of
Congress

ISBN 0-375-42082-7

www.pantheonbooks.com

Printed in the United States of America

First American Edition

9 8 7 6 5 4 3 2 1

For Michele Hutchison

Contents

DEPARTURE

I

On Anticipation

Places	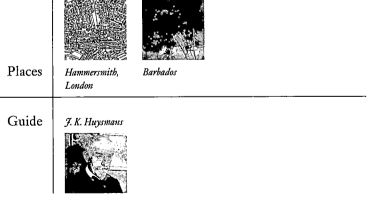*Hammersmith, London*	*Barbados*
Guide	*J. K. Huysmans*	

1.

It was hard to say when exactly winter arrived. The decline was gradual, like that of a person into old age, inconspicuous from day to day until the season became an established, relentless reality. First came a dip in evening temperatures, then days of continuous rain, confused gusts of Atlantic wind, dampness, the fall of leaves and the changing of the clocks—though there were still occasional moments of reprieve, mornings when one could leave the house without a coat and the sky was cloudless and bright. But they were like false signs of recovery in a patient upon whom death has already passed its sentence. By December the new season was entrenched, and the city was covered almost every day by an ominous steel-grey sky, like one in a painting by Mantegna or Veronese, the perfect backdrop to the crucifixion of Christ or to a day beneath the bedclothes. The neighbourhood park became a desolate spread of mud and water, lit up at night by rain-streaked street lamps. Passing it one evening during a downpour, I recalled how, in the intense heat of the previous summer, I had stretched out on the ground and let my bare feet slip out of my shoes to caress the grass, and how this direct contact with the earth had brought with it a sense of freedom and expansiveness, summer breaking down the usual boundaries between indoors and out and allowing me to feel as much at home in the world as in my own bedroom.

But now the park was foreign once more, the grass a forbidding arena in the incessant rain. Any sadness I might have felt, any suspicion that happiness or understanding was unattainable, seemed to find ready encouragement in the sodden dark-red brick buildings and low skies tinged orange by the city's streetlights.

William Hodges, *Tahiti Revisited*, 1776

Such climatic circumstances, together with a sequence of events that occurred at around this time (and seemed to confirm Chamfort's dictum that a man must swallow a toad every morning to be sure of not meeting with anything more revolting in the day ahead), conspired to render me intensely susceptible to the unsolicited arrival one late afternoon of a large, brightly illustrated brochure entitled 'Winter Sun'. Its cover displayed a row of palm trees, many of them growing at an angle, on a sandy beach fringed by a turquoise sea, set against a backdrop of hills where I imagined there to be waterfalls and relief from the heat in the shade of sweet-smelling fruit trees. The photographs reminded me of the paintings of Tahiti that William Hodges had brought back from his journey with Captain Cook, showing a tropical lagoon in soft evening light, where smiling local girls cavorted carefree (and barefoot) through luxuriant foliage—images that had provoked wonder and longing when Hodges had first exhibited them at the Royal Academy in London in the sharp winter of 1776, and that continued to provide a model for subsequent depictions of tropical idylls, including those in the pages of 'Winter Sun'.

Those responsible for the brochure had darkly intuited how easily their audience might be turned into prey by photographs whose power insulted the intelligence and contravened any notions of free will: overexposed photographs of palm trees, clear skies and white beaches. Readers who would have been capable of scepticism and prudence in other areas of their lives reverted, in contact with these elements, to a primordial innocence and optimism. The longing provoked by the brochure was an example, at once touching and bathetic, of how projects (and even whole lives) might be influenced by the simplest and most unexamined images of happiness; of how a lengthy and ruinously expensive journey might be set into motion by nothing more than the sight of a photograph of a palm tree gently inclining in a tropical breeze.

I resolved to travel to the island of Barbados.

2.

If our lives are dominated by a search for happiness, then perhaps few activities reveal as much about the dynamics of this quest—in all its ardour and paradoxes—than our travels. They express, however, inarticulately, an understanding of what life might be about, outside of the constraints of work and of the struggle for survival. Yet rarely are they considered to present philosophical problems—that is, issues requiring thought beyond the practical. We are inundated with advice on *where* to travel to, but we hear little of *why* and *how* we should go, even though the art of travel seems naturally to sustain a number of questions neither so simple nor so trivial, and whose study might in modest ways contribute to an understanding of what the Greek philosophers beautifully termed *eudaimonia,* or 'human flourishing'.

3.

One question revolves around the relationship between the anticipation of travel and its reality. I came upon a copy of J. K. Huysmans's novel *A Rebours,* published in 1884, whose effete and misanthropic hero, the aristocratic Duc des Esseintes, anticipated a journey to London and offered in the process an extravagantly pessimistic analysis of the difference between what we imagine about a place and what can occur when we reach it.

Huysmans recounts that the Duc des Esseintes lived alone in a vast villa on the outskirts of Paris. He rarely went anywhere to avoid what he took to be the ugliness and stupidity of others. One afternoon in his youth, he had ventured into a nearby village for a few hours and had felt his detestation of people grow fierce. Since then he had chosen to spend his days alone in bed in his study, reading the classics of literature and moulding acerbic thoughts about humanity. Early one morning, however, the duc surprised himself by experiencing an intense wish to travel to London. The desire came upon him as he sat by the fire reading a volume of Dickens. The book evoked visions of English life, which he contemplated at length and grew increasingly keen to see. Unable to contain his excitement, he ordered his servants to pack his bags, dressed himself in a grey tweed suit, a pair of laced ankle boots, a little bowler hat and a flax-blue Inverness cape and took the next train to Paris. With some time to spare before the departure of the London train, he stopped in at Galignani's English Bookshop on the Rue de Rivoli and there bought a volume of Baedeker's *Guide to London*. He was thrown into delicious reveries by its terse descriptions of the city's attractions. Next he moved on to a nearby wine bar frequented by a largely English clientele. The atmosphere was out of Dickens: he thought of scenes in which Little Dorrit, Dora Copperfield and Tom Pinch's sister Ruth sat in similarly cosy, bright rooms. One patron had Mr Wickfield's white hair and ruddy complexion, combined with the sharp, expressionless features and unfeeling eyes of Mr Tulkinghorn.

Hungry, des Esseintes went next to an English tavern in the Rue d'Amsterdam, near the Gare Saint Lazare. It was dark and smoky inside, with a line of beer pulls along a counter spread with hams as brown as violins and lobsters the colour of red lead. Seated at small wooden tables were robust Englishwomen with boyish faces, teeth as big as palette knives, cheeks as red as apples and long hands and feet. Des Esseintes found a table and ordered some oxtail soup, a smoked haddock, a helping of roast beef and potatoes, a couple of pints of ale and a chunk of Stilton.

But as the moment to board his train approached, along with the chance to turn his dreams of London into reality, des Esseintes was abruptly overcome with lassitude. He thought how wearing it would be actually to make the journey—how he would have to run to the station, fight for a porter, board the train, endure an unfamiliar bed, stand in lines, feel cold and move his fragile frame around the sights that Baedeker had so tersely described—and thus soil his dreams: 'What was the good of moving when a person could travel so wonderfully sitting in a chair? Wasn't he already in London, whose smells, weather, citizens, food, and even cutlery were all about him? What could he expect to find over there except fresh disappointments?' Still seated at his table, he reflected, 'I must have been suffering from some mental aberration to have rejected the visions of my obedient imagination and to have believed like any old ninny that it was necessary, interesting and useful to travel abroad.'

So des Esseintes paid the bill, left the tavern and took the first train back to his villa, along with his trunks, his packages, his portmanteaux, his rugs, his umbrellas and his sticks—and never left home again.

4.

We are familiar with the notion that the reality of travel is not what we anticipate. The pessimistic school, of which des Esseintes might be an honorary patron, therefore argues that reality must always be disappointing. It may be truer and more rewarding to suggest that it is primarily *different*.

After two months of anticipation, on a cloudless February mid-afternoon, I touched down, along with my travelling companion, M., at Barbados's Grantley Adams Airport. It was a short walk from the plane to the low airport buildings, but long enough to register a revolution in the climate. In only a few hours, I had travelled to a heat and a humidity that at home I would not have felt for another five months, and that even in midsummer there never achieved such intensity.

Nothing was as I had imagined it, which is surprising only if one considers *what* I had imagined. In the preceding weeks, my thoughts of the island had circled exclusively around three immobile mental images, assembled during the reading of a brochure and an airline timetable. The first image was of a beach with a palm tree against the setting sun. The second was of a hotel bungalow with a view through French doors into a room decorated with wooden floors and white bedlinen. And the third was of an azure sky.

If pressed, I would naturally have recognised that the island had to include other elements, but I had not needed them in order to build an impression of it. My behaviour was like that of a theatregoer who imagines without difficulty that the actions on stage are unfolding in Sherwood Forest or ancient Rome because the backdrop has been painted with a single branch of an oak or one Doric pillar.

But on my actual arrival, a range of things insisted that they, too, deserved to be included within the fold of the word *Barbados*. For example, a large petrol storage facility, decorated with the yellow and green logo of British Petroleum, and a small plywood box where an immigration official sat in an immaculate brown suit and gazed with an air of curiosity and unhurried wonder (like a scholar scanning the pages of a manuscript in the stacks of a library) at the passports of a line of tourists that began to stretch out of the terminal and onto the edge of the airfield. There was an advertisement for rum above the baggage carousel, a picture of the prime minister in the customs corridor, a *bureau de change* in the arrivals hall and a confusion of taxi drivers and tour guides outside the terminal building. And if there was a problem with this profusion of images, it was that they made it strangely harder for me to *see* the Barbados I had come to find.

In my anticipation, there had simply been a vacuum between the airport and my hotel. Nothing had existed in my mind between the last line on the itinerary (the beautifully rhythmic 'Arrival BA 2155 at 15.35') and the hotel room. I had not envisioned, and now protested inwardly the appearance of, a luggage carousel with a frayed rubber mat; two flies dancing above an overflowing ashtray; a giant fan turning inside the arrivals hall; a white taxi with a dashboard covered in fake leopard skin; a stray dog in a stretch of waste ground beyond the airport; an advertisement for 'luxury condos' at a roundabout; a factory called Bardak Electronics; a row of buildings with red and green tin roofs; a rubber strap on the central pillar of the car, upon which was written in very small print 'Volkswagen, Wolfsburg'; a brightly coloured bush whose name I didn't know; a hotel reception area that showed the time in six different locations and a card pinned on the wall nearby that read, with two months' delay, 'Merry Christmas'. Only several hours after my arrival did I find myself united with my imagined room, though I had had no prior mental image of its vast air-conditioning unit or, welcome though it might be in the event, its bathroom, which was made of Formica panels and had a notice sternly advising residents not to waste water.

If we are inclined to forget how much there is in the world besides that which we anticipate, then works of art are perhaps a little to blame, for in them we find at work the same process of simplification or selection as in the imagination. Artistic accounts involve severe abbreviations of what reality will force upon us. A travel book may tell us, for example, that the narrator journeyed through the afternoon to reach the hill town of X and after a night in its medieval monastery awoke to a misty dawn. But we never simply 'journey through an afternoon'. We sit in a train. Lunch digests awkwardly within us. The seat cloth is grey. We look out the window at a field. We look back inside. A drum of anxieties revolves in our consciousness. We notice a luggage label affixed to a suitcase in a rack above the seats opposite. We tap a finger on the window ledge. A broken nail on an index finger catches a thread. It starts to rain. A drop wends a muddy path down the dust-coated window. We wonder where our ticket might be. We look back out at the field. It continues to rain. At last the train starts to move. It passes an iron bridge, after which it inexplicably stops. A fly lands on the window. And still we may have reached the end only of the first minute of a comprehensive account of the events lurking within the deceptive sentence 'He journeyed through the afternoon'.

A storyteller who provided us with such a profusion of details would rapidly grow maddening. Unfortunately, life itself often subscribes to this mode of storytelling, wearing us out with repetitions, misleading emphases and inconsequential plot lines. It insists on showing us Bardak Electronics, the safety handle in the car, a stray dog, a Christmas card and a fly that lands first on the rim and then in the centre of a laden ashtray.

Which explains the curious phenomenon whereby valuable elements may be easier to experience in art and in anticipation than in reality. The anticipatory and artistic imaginations omit and compress; they cut away the periods of boredom and direct our attention to critical moments, and thus, without either lying or embellishing, they lend to life a vividness and a coherence that it may lack in the distracting woolliness of the present.

As I lay awake in bed on my first Caribbean night, thinking back over my journey (there were crickets and shufflings in the bushes outside), already the confusion of the present moment was receding, and certain events had begun to assume prominence, for memory is in this respect similar to anticipation: an instrument of simplification and selection.

The present might be compared to a long-winded film from which memory and anticipation select photographic highlights. Of my nine-and-a-half-hour flight to the island, active memory retained only six or seven static images. Just one survives today: the appearance of the in-flight tray. Of my experience at the airport, only an image of the passport line remained accessible. My layers of experience had settled into a compact and well-defined narrative: I became a man who had flown in from London and checked into his hotel.

I fell asleep early and the next morning awoke to my first Caribbean dawn—though there was, inevitably, a lot more beneath these brisk words than that.

5.

There was one other country that, many years before his intended trip to England, des Esseintes had wanted to see: Holland. He had imagined the place to resemble the paintings of Teniers and Jan Steen, Rembrandt and Ostade; he had anticipated patriarchal simplicity and riotous joviality, quiet small brick courtyards and pale-faced maids pouring milk. And so he had journeyed to Haarlem and Amsterdam—and was greatly disappointed. The problem was not

Jacob Isaacksz van Ruisdael, *View of Alkmaar, c.* 1670–75

that the paintings themselves lied—the place did offer some simplicity and joviality, some nice brick courtyards and a few serving women pouring milk—but rather that the promised gems were blended in a stew of ordinary images (restaurants, offices, uniform houses and featureless fields) that the Dutch artists had never painted, and that made the experience of travelling in the country seem strangely diluted compared with an afternoon spent in the Dutch galleries of the Louvre, where the essence of Dutch beauty found itself collected in just a few rooms.

Des Esseintes thus ended up in the paradoxical position of feeling more *in* Holland—that is, more intensely in contact with the elements he loved in Dutch culture—when looking at selected images of Holland in a museum than when travelling with sixteen pieces of luggage and two servants through the country itself.

6.

Awakening early that first morning, I slipped on a dressing gown provided by the hotel and went out onto the veranda. In the dawn light, the sky was a pale grey-blue, and after the rustlings of the night before, all the creatures and even the wind seemed in deep sleep. It was as quiet as a library. Beyond the hotel room stretched a wide beach whose fringe of coconut trees soon gave way to an unhindered sandy slope towards the sea. I climbed over the veranda's low railing and walked across the sand. Nature was at her most benevolent. It was as if, in creating this small horseshoe bay, she had chosen to atone for her ill temper in other regions and decided for once to display only her munificence. The coconut trees provided shade and milk, the floor of the sea was lined with shells, the sand was powdery and the colour of sun-ripened wheat, and the air—even in the shade—had an enveloping, profound warmth to it so unlike the fragility of northern European heat, always prone to cede, even in midsummer, to a more assertive, proprietary chill.

I found a deck chair at the edge of the sea. I could hear small lapping sounds beside me, as if a kindly monster were taking discreet sips of water from a large goblet. A few birds were waking up and beginning to career through the air in matinal excitement. Behind me, the raffia roofs of the hotel bungalows were visible through gaps in the trees. Before me was a view that I recognised from the brochure: the beach stretching away in a gentle curve towards the tip of the bay, with jungle-covered hills behind, and the first row of coconut trees inclining irregularly towards the turquoise sea, as though some of them were craning their necks to catch a better angle of the sun.

Yet this description only imperfectly reflects what occurred within me that morning, for my attention was in truth far more fractured and confused than the foregoing paragraphs suggest. I may have noticed a few birds careering through the air in matinal excitement, but my awareness of them was weakened by a number of other, incongruous and unrelated elements, among them a sore throat I had developed during the flight, worry over not having informed a colleague that I would be away, a pressure across both temples and a rising need to visit the bathroom. A momentous but until then overlooked fact was making itself apparent: I had inadvertently brought myself with me to the island.

It is easy for us to forget ourselves when we contemplate pictorial and verbal descriptions of places. At home, as my eyes had panned over photographs of Barbados, there were no reminders that those eyes were intimately tied to a body and mind that would travel with me wherever I went and that might, over time, assert their presence in ways that would threaten or even negate the purpose of what the

eyes had come there to see. At home I could concentrate on pictures of a hotel room, a beach or a sky and ignore the complex creature in which this observation was taking place and for whom it was only a small part of a larger, more multifaceted task of living.

My body and mind were to prove temperamental accomplices in the mission of appreciating my destination. The body found it hard to sleep and complained of heat, flies and difficulties digesting hotel meals. The mind meanwhile revealed a commitment to anxiety, boredom, free-floating sadness and financial alarm.

It seems that unlike the continuous, enduring contentment that we anticipate, our actual happiness with, and in, a place must be a brief and, at least to the conscious mind, apparently haphazard phenomenon: an interval in which we achieve receptivity to the world around us, in which positive thoughts of past and future coagulate and anxieties are allayed. The condition rarely endures for longer than ten minutes. New patterns of anxiety inevitably form on the horizon of consciousness, like the weather fronts that mass themselves every few days off the western coasts of Ireland. The past victory ceases to seem so impressive, the future acquires complications and the beautiful view becomes as invisible as anything which is always around.

I was to discover an unexpected continuity between the melancholic self I had been at home and the person I was to be on the island, a continuity quite at odds with the radical discontinuity in the landscape and climate, where the very air seemed to be made of a different and sweeter substance.

At midmorning on that first day, M. and I sat on deck chairs outside our beach hut. A single cloud hung shyly above the bay. M. put on her headphones and began annotating Emile Durkheim's *On Suicide*. I looked around me. It would have seemed to observers that I was where I lay. But 'I'—that is, the conscious part of my self—had in truth abandoned the physical envelope in which it dwelt in order to worry about the future, or more specifically about the issue of whether lunches would be included in the price of the room. Two hours later, seated at a corner table in the hotel restaurant with a papaya (lunch and local taxes included), the I that had left my body on the deck chair now made another migration, quitting the island altogether to visit a troubling project scheduled for the following year.

It was as if a vital evolutionary advantage had been bestowed centuries ago on those members of the species who lived in a state of concern about what was to happen next. These ancestors might have failed to savour their experiences appropriately, but they had at least survived and shaped the character of their descendants, while their more focused siblings, at one with the moment and with the place where they stood, had met violent ends on the horns of unforeseen bison.

It is unfortunately hard to recall our quasi-permanent concern with the future, for on our return from a place, perhaps the first thing to disappear from memory is just how much of the past we spent dwelling on what was to come—how much of it, that is, we spent somewhere other than where we were. There is a purity both in the remembered and in the anticipated visions of a place: in each instance it is the place itself that is allowed to stand out.

If fidelity to a place had seemed possible from home, it was perhaps because I had never tried to stare at a picture of Barbados for any length of time. Had I laid one on a table and forced myself to look at it exclusively for twenty-five minutes, my mind and body would naturally have migrated towards a range of extrinsic concerns, and I might thereby have gained a more accurate sense of how little the place in which I stood had the power to influence what travelled through my mind.

In another paradox that des Esseintes would have appreciated, it seems we may best be able to inhabit a place when we are not faced with the additional challenge of having to be there.

7.

A few days before the end of our stay, M. and I decided to explore the island. We rented a Mini Moke and headed north to an area of rugged hills called Scotland, to which Oliver Cromwell had exiled English Catholics in the seventeenth century. At Barbados's northernmost tip, we visited Animal Flower Cave, a series of caverns hollowed out of the rock face by the pounding of the waves. Giant sea anemones grew along the pitted walls there, looking like yellow and green flowers when they opened their tendrils.

At midday we headed south towards the parish of Saint John and there, on a tree-covered hill, found a restaurant in one wing of an old colonial mansion. In the garden were a cannonball tree and an African tulip tree, the latter with flowers in the shape of upside-down trumpets. A leaflet informed us that the house and gardens had been built by the administrator Sir Anthony Hutchison in 1745 and had cost the apparently enormous trade of a hundred thousand pounds of sugar. Ten tables were set out along a gallery, with a view of the gardens and the sea. We took our place at the far end, beside an efflorescent bougainvillea bush. M. ordered jumbo shrimp in sweet pepper sauce, and I had a kingfish with onions and herbs in red wine. We talked about the colonial system and the curious ineffectiveness of even the most powerful sunblocks. For dessert, we ordered two crèmes caramel.

When the crèmes arrived, M. was given a large but messy portion that looked as if it had fallen over in the kitchen, and I a tiny but perfectly formed one. As soon as the waiter had stepped out of eyeshot, M. reached over and swapped my plate for hers.

'Don't steal my dessert,' I said, incensed.

'I thought you wanted the bigger one,' she replied, no less affronted.

'You're just trying to get the better one.'

'I'm not; I'm trying to be nice to you. Stop being suspicious.'

'I will if you give me back my portion.'

In only a few moments, we had plunged into a shameful interlude where beneath infantile rounds of bickering there stirred mutual terrors of incompatibility and infidelity.

M. handed back my plate grimly, took a few spoons from hers and pushed the dessert to one side. We said nothing. We paid and drove back to the hotel, the sound of the engine disguising the intensity of our sulks. The room had been cleaned in our absence. The bed had fresh linen. There were flowers on the chest of drawers and new beach towels in the bathroom. I tore one from the pile and went to sit on the veranda, closing the French doors violently behind me. The coconut trees were throwing a gentle shade, the crisscross patterns of their palms occasionally rearranging themselves in the afternoon breeze. But there was no pleasure for me in such beauty. I had enjoyed nothing aesthetic or material since the struggle over the crèmes caramel several hours before. It had become irrelevant that there were soft towels, flowers and attractive views. My mood refused to be lifted by any external prop; it even felt insulted by the perfection of the weather and the prospect of the beachside barbecue scheduled for that evening.

Our misery that afternoon, in which the smell of tears mixed with the scents of sun cream and air conditioning, was a reminder of the rigid, unforgiving logic to which human moods appear to be subject, a logic that we ignore at our peril when we encounter a picture of a beautiful land and imagine that happiness must naturally accompany such magnificence. Our capacity to draw happiness from aesthetic objects or material goods in fact seems critically dependent on our first satisfying a more important range of emotional or psychological needs, among them the need for understanding, for love, expression and respect. Thus we will not enjoy—we are not *able* to enjoy—sumptuous tropical gardens and attractive wooden beach huts when a relationship to which we are committed abruptly reveals itself to be suffused with incomprehension and resentment.

If we are surprised by the power of one sulk to destroy the beneficial effects of an entire hotel, it is because we misunderstand what holds up our moods. We are sad at home and blame the weather and the ugliness of the buildings, but on the tropical island we learn (after an argument in a raffia bungalow under an azure sky) that the state of the skies and the appearance of our dwellings can never on their own either underwrite our joy or condemn us to misery.

There is a contrast between the vast projects we set in motion, the construction of hotels and the dredging of bays, and the basic psychological knots that undermine them. How quickly may the advantages of civilisation be wiped out by a tantrum. The intractability of the mental knots points to the austere, wry wisdom of those ancient philosophers who walked away from prosperity and sophistication and argued, from within a barrel or a mud hut, that the key ingredients of happiness could not be material or aesthetic but must always be stubbornly psychological—a lesson that never seemed truer than when M. and I made up at nightfall, in the shadow of a beachside barbecue whose luxury had become a humbling irrelevance.

8.

After Holland and his abortive visit to England, des Esseintes did not attempt another journey abroad. He remained in his villa and surrounded himself with a series of objects that facilitated the finest aspect of travel: its anticipation. He had coloured prints hung on his walls, like those in travel agents' windows, showing foreign cities, museums, hotels and steamers bound for Valparaiso or the River Plate. He had the itineraries of the major shipping companies framed, and lined his bedroom with them. He filled an aquarium with seaweed, bought a sail, some rigging and a pot of tar, and with their help was able to experience the most pleasant aspects of a long sea voyage without any of its inconveniences. Des Esseintes concluded, in Huysmans's words, that 'the imagination could provide a more-than-adequate substitute for the vulgar reality of actual experience'. Actual experience where what we have come to see is always diluted in what we could see anywhere, where we are drawn away from the present by an anxious future and where our appreciation of aesthetic elements lies at the mercy of perplexing physical and psychological demands.

I travelled in spite of des Esseintes. And yet there were times when I, too, felt that there might be no finer journeys than those provoked in the imagination by remaining at home slowly turning the Bible-paper pages of the British Airways Worldwide Timetable.

II

On Travelling Places

Places	*The service station*	*The airport*	*The plane*	*The train*
Guides	*Charles Baudelaire*	*Edward Hopper*		

1.

Overlooking the motorway between London and Manchester, in a flat, featureless expanse of country, stands a single-storey glass-and-redbrick service station. In its forecourt hangs a giant laminated flag that advertises to motorists and to the sheep in an adjacent field a photograph of a fried egg, two sausages and a peninsula of baked beans.

I arrived at the service station towards evening. The sky was turning red in the West, and in a row of ornamental trees to the side of the building, birds could be heard against the incessant bass note of the traffic. I had been on the road for two hours, alone with clouds forming on the horizon, with the lights of commuter towns beyond the grass banks, with motorway bridges and the silhouettes of overtaking cars and coaches. I felt dizzy stepping out of my craft, which gave off a series of clicks as it cooled, as if paper clips were being dropped through the bonnet. My senses needed to readjust themselves to firm land, to the wind and to the discreet sounds of night drawing in.

The restaurant was brightly illuminated and exaggeratedly warm. Large photographs of coffee cups, pastries and hamburgers hung on the walls. A waitress was refilling a drinks dispenser. I slid a damp tray along a metal runway, bought a bar of chocolate and an orange juice and sat by a window that made up one wall of the building. Vast panes were held in place by strips of beige putty, into whose chewy clamminess I was tempted to dig my nails. Beyond the window, the grass sloped down to the motorway, where traffic ran in silent, elegant symmetry along six lanes, the differences in makes and colours of cars disguised by the gathering darkness, leaving a uniform ribbon of red and white diamonds extending into infinity in two directions.

There were few other customers in the service station. A woman was idly rotating a teabag in a cup. A man and two small girls were eating hamburgers. A bearded elderly man was doing a crossword. No one was talking. There was an air of reflection, of sadness, too— only heightened by the faint sound of piped upbeat music and the enamel smile of a woman about to bite into a bacon sandwich in a photograph above the counter. In the middle of the room, hanging from the ceiling and dancing nervously in the breeze of an air vent, was a cardboard box announcing an offer of free onion rings with every hot dog. Misshapen and upside down, the box seemed only a rough approximation of what head office must have stipulated, like those milestones in distant parts of the Roman Empire whose form strayed from the designs of the centre.

The building was architecturally miserable, it smelt of frying oil and lemon-scented floor polish, the food was glutinous and the tables were dotted with islands of dried ketchup from the meals of long-departed travellers, yet something about the scene moved me. There was poetry in this forsaken service station perched on the ridge of the motorway, far from all habitation. Its appeal made me think of certain other equally and unexpectedly poetic travelling places—airport terminals, harbours, train stations and motels—and the work of a nineteenth-century writer and a twentieth-century painter he inspired, who were, in their different ways, unusually alive to the power of the liminal travelling place.

2.

Charles Baudelaire was born in Paris in 1821. From an early age, he felt uncomfortable at home. His father died when he was five, and a year later his mother married a man her son disliked. He was sent to a succession of boarding schools from which he was repeatedly expelled for insubordination. As an adult, he could find no place in bourgeois society. He quarrelled with his mother and stepfather, wore theatrical black capes and hung reproductions of Delacroix's *Hamlet* lithographs around his bedroom. In his diary, he complained of suffering from 'that appalling disease: the Horror of Home' and from a 'feeling of loneliness, from earliest childhood. Despite the family—and with school friends especially—a feeling of being destined to lead an eternally solitary life.'

He dreamt of leaving France for somewhere else, somewhere far away, on another continent, with no reminders of 'the everyday' (a term of horror for the poet)—somewhere with warmer weather, a place, in the words of the legendary couplet from *L'Invitation au Voyage*, where everything would be '*ordre et beauté/Luxe, calme et volupté*'. But he was aware of the difficulties involved. He had once left the leaden skies of northern France and returned dejected. He had set off on a journey to India. Three months into the sea crossing, the ship had run into a storm and had stopped in Mauritius for repairs. It was the lush, palm-fringed island that Baudelaire had dreamt of. But he could not shake off a feeling of lethargy and sadness, and he suspected that India would be no better. Despite efforts by the captain to persuade him otherwise, he insisted on sailing back to France.

The result was a lifelong ambivalence towards travel. In *Le Voyage*, he sarcastically imagined the accounts of travellers returned from afar:

We saw stars
And waves; we saw sands, too;

And despite many crises and unforeseen disasters,
We were often bored, just as we are here.

And yet he remained sympathetic to the wish to travel and observed its tenacious hold on him. No sooner had he returned to Paris from his Mauritian trip than he began to dream once again of going somewhere else. Noting, 'Life is a hospital in which every patient is obsessed with changing beds: this one wants to suffer in front of the radiator, and that one thinks he'd get better if he was by the window,' he was nevertheless unashamed to count himself among the patients: 'It always seems to me that I'll be well where I am not, and this question of moving is one that I'm forever entertaining with my soul.' Sometimes Baudelaire dreamt of going to Lisbon. It would be warm there, and he would, like a lizard, gain strength from stretching himself out in the sun. It was a city of water, marble and light, conducive to thought and calm. But almost from the moment he conceived this Portuguese fantasy, he would start to wonder if he might not be happier in Holland. Then again, why not Java or the Baltic or even the North Pole, where he could bathe in shadows and watch comets fly across the Arctic skies? The destination was not really the point. The true desire was to get away—to go, as he concluded, 'anywhere! anywhere! so long as it is out of the world!'

Baudelaire honoured reveries of travel as a mark of those noble, questing souls whom he described as 'poets', who could not be satisfied with the horizons of home even as they appreciated the limits of other lands, whose temperaments oscillated between hope and despair, childlike idealism and cynicism. It was the fate of poets, like Christian pilgrims, to live in a fallen world while refusing to surrender their vision of an alternative, less compromised realm.

Against such ideas, one detail stands out in Baudelaire's biography: he was, throughout his life, strongly drawn to harbours, docks, railway stations, trains, ships and hotel rooms, and felt more at home in the transient places of travel than in his own dwelling. When he was oppressed by the atmosphere in Paris, when the world seemed 'monotous and small', he would leave, 'leave for leaving's sake', and travel to a harbour or train station, where he would inwardly exclaim:

> *Carriage, take me with you! Ship, steal me away from here!*
> *Take me far, far away. Here the mud is made of our tears!*

In an essay on the poet, T. S. Eliot proposed that Baudelaire was the first nineteenth-century artist to give expression to the beauty of modern travelling places and machines. 'Baudelaire...invented a new kind of romantic nostalgia,' wrote Eliot: 'the *poésie des départs*, the *poésie des salles d'attente.*' And, one might add, the *poésie des stations-service* and the *poésie des aéroports.*

3.

When feeling sad at home, I have often boarded a train or airport bus and gone to Heathrow, where, from an observation gallery in Terminal 2 or from the top floor of the Renaissance Hotel along the north runway, I have drawn comfort from the sight of the ceaseless landings and takeoffs of aircraft.

In the difficult year of 1859, in the aftermath of the *Fleurs du Mal* trial and his breakup with his mistress Jeanne Duval, Baudelaire visited his mother at her home in Honfleur and, for much of his two-month stay, occupied a chair at the quayside, watching vessels docking and departing. 'Those large and beautiful ships, invisibly balanced (hovering) on tranquil waters, those hardy ships that look dreamy and idle, don't they seem to whisper to us in silent tongues: 'When shall we set sail for happiness?'

Seen from a car park beside 09L/27R, as the north runway is known to pilots, the 747 appears at first as a small, brilliant white light, a star dropping towards earth. It has been in the air for twelve hours. It took off from Singapore in the late morning. It flew over the Bay of Bengal, Delhi, the Afghan desert and the Caspian Sea. It traced a course over Romania, the Czech Republic and southern Germany before beginning its descent, so gently that few passengers would have even noticed a change of tone in the engines, above the grey-brown, turbulent waters off the Dutch coast. It followed the Thames over London, turned north near Hammersmith (where the flaps began to unfold), pivoted over Uxbridge and straightened course over Slough. From the ground, the white light gradually takes shape as a vast, two-storeyed body with four engines suspended like earrings beneath implausibly long wings. In the light rain, clouds of water form a veil behind the plane on its matronly progress towards the airfield. Beneath it are the suburbs of Slough. It is three in the afternoon. In detached villas, kettles are being filled. A television is on in a living room, its sound switched off. Green and red shadows move silently across walls. The everyday. And above Slough is a plane that a few hours ago was flying over the Caspian Sea. Slough/the Caspian: the plane a symbol of worldliness, carrying within itself a trace of all the lands it has crossed, its eternal mobility offering an imaginative counterweight to feelings of stagnation and confinement.

This morning the plane was over the Malay Peninsula, a place-name in which there linger the smells of guava and sandalwood. And

now, a few metres above the earth that it has avoided for so long, the plane appears motionless, its nose raised upwards, seeming to pause before its sixteen rear wheels meet the tarmac with a blast of smoke that makes manifest its speed and weight.

On a parallel runway, an A340 ascends for New York and, over the Staines Reservoir, retracts its flaps and wheels, which it won't require again until the descent over the white clapboard houses of Long Beach, three thousand miles and eight hours of sea-and-cloud away. Visible through the heat haze of turbofans, other planes wait to start their journeys. All across the airfield, planes are on the move, their fins a confusion of colours against the grey horizon, like sails at a regatta.

Along the glass-and-steel back of Terminal 3 rest four giants, whose liveries indicate a varied provenance: Canada, Brazil, Pakistan, Korea. For a few hours their wingtips will lie only a few metres apart, until each set begins another journey into the stratospheric winds. As every ship turns into a gate, a choreographed dance begins. Trucks slip to the underbelly, black fuel hoses are fastened to the wings, a gangway bends its rectangular rubber lips over the fuselage. The doors of the holds are opened to disgorge battered aluminium cargo crates, perhaps containing fruit that only a few days ago hung from the branches of tropical trees, or vegetables that had their roots in the soil of high, silent valleys. Two men in overalls set up a small ladder next to one engine and open up its casing to reveal an intricate terrain of wires and small steel pipes. Sheets and pillows are lowered from the front of one cabin. Passengers disembark; for them this ordinary English afternoon will have a supernatural tinge.

Nowhere is the appeal of the airport more concentrated than in the television screens that hang in rows from the terminal ceilings to announce the departure and arrival of flights, whose absence of aesthetic self-consciousness and whose workmanlike casing and pedestrian typefaces do nothing to disguise their emotional charge and imaginative allure. Tokyo, Amsterdam, Istanbul, Warsaw, Seattle, Rio. The screens bear all the poetic resonance of the last line of James Joyce's *Ulysses*, which is at once a record of where the novel was written and, no less important, a symbol of the cosmopolitan spirit behind its composition: 'Trieste, Zurich, Paris.' The constant calls of the screens, some accompanied by the impatient pulsing of a cursor, suggest with what ease our seemingly entrenched lives might be altered were we simply to walk down a corridor and onto a craft that in a few hours would land us in a place of which we had no memories and where no one knew our name. How pleasant to hold in mind through the crevasses of our moods, at three in the afternoon, when lassitude and despair threaten, that there is always a plane taking off for somewhere, for Baudelaire's 'anywhere! anywhere!': Trieste, Zurich, Paris.

4.

Baudelaire admired not only the places of departure and arrival but also the machines of motion, and in particular oceangoing ships. He wrote, for example, of the 'profound and mysterious charm that arises from looking at a ship'. He went to see the flat-bottomed boats, or *caboteurs*, in the Port Saint Nicolas in Paris, and larger ships in Rouen and the Normandy ports. He marvelled at the technological achievements behind them, at how objects so heavy and multifarious could be made to move with elegance and cohesion across the seas. A great ship made him think of 'a vast, immense, complicated but agile creature, an animal full of spirit, suffering and heaving all the sighs and ambitions of humanity'.

We may feel similar sentiments upon looking at some of the

larger species of aeroplanes, themselves 'vast' and 'complicated' creatures, which defy their size and the chaos of the lower atmosphere to steer serenely across the firmament. On seeing such a thing parked at a gate, dwarfing luggage carts and mechanics, one is induced to feel surprise, overriding any scientific explanation, that it can move even a few metres, let alone fly to Japan. Buildings, among the few man-made structures of comparable size, do not prepare us for the aeroplane's agility or self-possession, for buildings may be cracked by slight movements of the earth, and they leak air and water and can lose parts of themselves to the wind.

Few seconds in life are more releasing than those in which a plane ascends to the sky. Looking out a window from inside a machine standing stationary at the beginning of a runway, we face a vista of familiar proportions: a road, oil cylinders, grass and hotels with copper-tinted windows—the earth as we have always known it, where we make slow progress, even with the help of a car, where calf muscles and engines strain to reach the summit of hills, where, half a mile ahead or less, there is almost always a line of trees or buildings to restrict our view. Then suddenly, accompanied by the controlled rage of the engines (with only a slight tremor from glasses in the galley), we rise fluently into the atmosphere, and an immense horizon opens up across which we can wander without impediment. A journey that on earth would have taken an afternoon can be accomplished with an infinitesimal movement of the eye; we can cross Berkshire, visit Maidenhead, skirt over Bracknell and survey the M4.

There is psychological pleasure in this takeoff, too, for the swiftness of the plane's ascent is an exemplary symbol of transformation. The display of power can inspire us to imagine analogous, decisive shifts in our own lives, to imagine that we, too, might one day surge above much that now looms over us.

The new vantage point lends order and logic to the landscape: roads curve to avoid hills, rivers trace paths to lakes, pylons lead from power stations to towns, streets that from earth seemed laid out without thought emerge as well-planned grids. The eye attempts to match what it can see with what the mind knows should be there, like a reader trying to decipher a familiar book in a new language. Those lights must be Newbury, that road the A33 as it leaves the M4. And to think that all along, hidden from our sight, our lives were that small: the world we live in but almost never see, the way we must appear to the hawk and to the gods.

The plane's engines show none of the effort required to take us to this place. They hang there in the inconceivable cold, patiently and invisibly powering the craft, their sole requests, painted on their inner flanks in red letters, being that we do not walk on them and that we feed them 'Oil only: D50TFI-S4', a message for a forthcoming set of men in overalls, 4,000 miles away and still asleep.

There is not much talk about the clouds that are visible up here. No one seems to think it remarkable that somewhere above an ocean we are flying past a vast white candy-floss island that would have made a perfect seat for an angel or even God himself in a painting by Piero della Francesca. In the cabin, no one stands up to announce with requisite emphasis that if we look out the window, we will see that *we are flying over a cloud,* a matter that would have detained Leonardo and Poussin, Claude and Constable.

Food that if sampled in a kitchen would have been banal or even offensive acquires a new taste and interest in the presence of the clouds (like a picnic of bread and cheese that delights us when we

eat it on a clifftop above a pounding sea). With the in-flight tray, we make ourselves at home in this unhomely place: we appropriate the extraterrestrial landscape with the help of a chilled bread roll and a plastic dish of potato salad.

When scrutinised, our airborne companions outside the window do not look as we might expect them to. In paintings and from the ground, they appear to be horizontal ovoids, but up here they resemble giant obelisks made of piles of unsteady shaving foam. Their kinship with steam becomes clearer: they seem more volatile, perhaps the product of something that has just exploded and is still mutating. It remains perplexing that it should be impossible to sit on one.

Baudelaire knew how to love the clouds.

THE OUTSIDER

Tell me, whom do you love most, you enigmatic man: your father, your mother, your sister or your brother?

I have neither father, nor mother, nor sister, nor brother.

Your friends?

You're using a word I've never understood.

Your country?

I don't know where that might lie.

Beauty?

I would love her with all my heart, if only she were a goddess and immortal.

Money?

I hate it as you hate God.

Well, then, what do you love, you strange outsider?

I love the clouds ... the clouds that pass by ... over there ... over there ... those lovely clouds!

The clouds usher in tranquillity. Below us are enemies and colleagues, the sites of our terrors and our griefs, all of them now infinitesimal, mere scratches on the earth. We may know this old lesson in perspective well enough, but rarely does it seem as true as when we are pressed against the cold plane window, our craft a teacher of profound philosophy and a faithful disciple of the Baudelairean command:

> *Carriage, take me with you! Ship, steal me away from here!*
> *Take me far, far away. Here the mud is made of our tears!*

5.

There was, apart from the motorway, no road linking the service station to other places—not even a footpath. It seemed to belong not to the city, nor to the country, either, but rather to some third, travellers' realm, like a lighthouse at the edge of the ocean.

This geographical isolation enforced the atmosphere of solitude in the dining area. The lighting was unforgiving, bringing out pallor and blemishes. The chairs and seats, painted in childishly bright colours, had the strained jollity of a fake smile. No one was talking, no one admitting to curiosity or fellow feeling. We gazed blankly past one another at the serving counter or out into the darkness. We might have been seated among rocks.

I remained in one corner, eating fingers of chocolate and taking occasional sips of orange juice. I felt lonely, but for once it was a gentle, even pleasant kind of loneliness, because rather than unfolding against a backdrop of laughter and fellowship, which would have caused me to suffer from the contrast between my mood and the environment, it had as its locus a place where everyone was a stranger, where the difficulties of communication and the frustrated longing for love seemed to be acknowledged and brutally celebrated by the architecture and lighting.

The collective loneliness brought to mind certain canvases by Edward Hopper, which, despite the bleakness they depict, are not themselves bleak to look at but rather allow the viewer to witness an echo of his or her own grief and thereby to feel less personally persecuted and beset by it. It is perhaps sad books that best console us when we are sad, and to lonely service stations that we should drive when there is no one for us to hold or love.

In 1906, at the age of twenty-four, Hopper went to Paris, where he discovered the poetry of Baudelaire. He was to read and recite the Frenchman's work throughout his life. The attraction is not hard to understand: the two men had shared interests in solitude, in city life, in modernity, in the solace of the night and in the places of travel. In 1925, Hopper bought his first car, a secondhand Dodge, and drove from his home in New York to New Mexico; from that point on he spent several months on the road every year, sketching and painting along the way, in motel rooms, in the backs of cars, outdoors and in diners. Between 1941 and 1955, he crossed America five times. He stayed in Best Western motels, Del Haven cabins, Alamo Plaza courts and Blue Top lodges. He was drawn to the sorts of places whose neon signs blink 'Vacancy, TV, Bath' from the side of the road, offering beds with thin mattresses and crisp sheets, large windows overlooking car parks or small patches of manicured lawn, the mystery of guests who arrive late and set off at dawn, brochures for local attractions in the reception area and laden housekeeping trolleys parked in silent corridors. For meals Hopper would stop at diners, at Hot Shoppes Mighty Mo Drive-Ins, Steak 'N' Shakes or Dog 'N' Suds, and he would fill up his car at petrol stations displaying the logos of Mobil, Standard Oil, Gulf and Blue Sunoco.

And in these ignored, often derided landscapes, Hopper found poetry: the *poésie des motels*, the *poésie des petits restaurants au bord d'une route*. His paintings (and their resonant titles) suggest a consistent interest in five different kinds of travelling places:

1. HOTELS
   Hotel Room (1931)
   Hotel Lobby (1943)
   Rooms for Tourists (1945)
   Hotel by a Railroad (1952)
   Hotel Window (1956)
   Western Motel (1957)

2. ROADS AND PETROL STATIONS
   Road in Maine (1914)
   Gas (1940)
   Route 6, Eastham (1941)
   Solitude (1944)
   Four-Lane Road (1956)

3. DINERS AND CAFETERIAS
   Automat (1927)
   Sunlight in a Cafeteria (1958)

4. VIEWS FROM TRAINS
   House by the Railroad (1925)
   New York, New Haven and Hartford (1931)
   Railroad Embankment (1932)
   Toward Boston (1936)

Approaching a City (1946)
Road and Trees (1962)

5. VIEWS INSIDE TRAINS AND OF ROLLING STOCK
Night on the El Train (1920)
Locomotive (1925)
Compartment C, Car 293 (1938)
Dawn in Pennsylvania (1942)
Chair Car (1965)

Loneliness is the dominant theme here. Hopper's figures seem far from home; they sit or stand alone, looking at a letter on the edge of a hotel bed or drinking in a bar, gazing out the window of a moving train or reading a book in a hotel lobby. Their faces are vulnerable and introspective. Having perhaps just left someone or been left themselves, they are in search of work, sex or company, adrift in transient places. It is often night, and through the window come the darkness and threat of the open country or of a strange city.

In *Automat* (1927), a woman sits alone drinking a cup of coffee. It is late and, to judge by her hat and coat, cold outside. The room seems large, brightly lit and empty. The decor is functional, with a stone-topped table, hard-wearing black wooden chairs and white walls. The woman looks self-conscious and slightly afraid, unused to sitting alone in a public place. Something appears to have gone wrong. She unwittingly invites the viewer to imagine stories for her, stories of betrayal or loss. She is trying not to let her hand shake as she moves the coffee cup to her lips. It may be eleven at night in February in a large North American city.

Automat is a picture of sadness, and yet it is not a sad picture. It has

Edward Hopper, *Automat*, 1927

the power of a great melancholy piece of music. Despite the stark-ness of the furnishings, the location itself does not seem wretched. Others in the room may be on their own as well, men and women drinking coffee by themselves, similarly lost in thought, similarly distanced from society: a common isolation that generally has the beneficial effect of lessening the oppressive sense within any one person that he or she is alone in being alone. In roadside diners and late-night cafeterias, hotel lobbies and station cafés, we may dilute our feeling of isolation in a lonely public place and hence rediscover a distinctive sense of community. The lack of domesticity, the bright lights and anonymous furniture may come as a relief from what are often the false comforts of home. It may be easier to give way to sad-ness here than in a living room with wallpaper and framed photos, the decor of a refuge that has let us down.

Hopper invites us to feel empathy with the woman in her isola-tion. She seems dignified and generous, only perhaps a little too trusting, a little naive—as if she has knocked against a hard corner of the world. Hopper puts us on her side, the side of the outsider against the insiders. The figures in Hopper's art are not opponents of home per se; it is simply that in a variety of undefined ways, home appears to have betrayed them, forcing them out into the night or onto the road. The twenty-four-hour diner, the station waiting room and the motel are sanctuaries for those who have, for noble reasons, failed to find a home in the ordinary world—those whom Baude-laire might have dignified with the honorific *poets*.

6.

As the car slips along a winding road through the woods at dusk, its powerful headlamps momentarily light up whole sections of meadow and tree trunks—so brightly that the texture of the bark and individual stalks of grass can be made out in a clinical white light better suited to a hospital ward than to woodland—and then dip them back into the undifferentiated murkiness as the car rounds the corner and the beams turn their attention to another patch of slumbering ground.

There are few other cars on the road, only an occasional set of lights moving in the opposite direction, away from the night. The car's instrument panel casts a purple glow over the darkened interior. Suddenly, in a clearing ahead, a floodlit expanse appears: a petrol station, the last before the road heads off into the longest, densest stretch of forest, and night completes its hold over the land—*Gas* (1940).

The manager has left his cabin to check the level on a pump. It is warm inside, and light as brilliant as that given off by the midday sun washes across the forecourt. A radio may be playing. There may be cans of oil neatly lined up against one wall, along with sweets, magazines, maps and window cloths.

Like *Automat*, painted thirteen years before it, *Gas* is a picture of isolation: a petrol station stands on its own in the impending darkness. But in Hopper's hands, the isolation is once again made poignant and enticing. The darkness that spreads like a fog from the right of the canvas, a harbinger of fear, contrasts with the security of the station itself. Against the backdrop of night and wild woods, in this last outpost of humanity, a sense of kinship may be easier to develop than in daylight in the city. The coffee machine and magazines, tokens of small human desires and vanities, stand in opposition to the wide nonhuman world outside, to the miles of forest in which branches crack now and then under the footfalls of bears and foxes. There is something touching in the suggestion—made in bold pink on the cover of one magazine—that we paint our nails purple

Edward Hopper, *Gas*, 1940

this summer, and in the imprecation above the coffee machine to sample the aroma of freshly roasted beans. At this last stop before the road enters the endless forest, what we have in common with others can loom larger than what separates us.

7.

Hopper also took an interest in trains. He was drawn to the atmosphere inside half-empty carriages making their way across a landscape: the silence that reigns inside while the wheels beat in rhythm against the rails outside, the dreaminess fostered by the noise and the view from the windows—a dreaminess in which we seem to stand outside our normal selves and to have access to thoughts and memories that may not arise in more settled circumstances. The woman in *Compartment C, Car 293* (1938) seems in such a frame of mind, reading her book and shifting her gaze between the carriage and the view.

Journeys are the midwives of thought. Few places are more conducive to internal conversations than moving planes, ships or trains. There is an almost quaint correlation between what is before our eyes and the thoughts we are able to have in our heads: large thoughts at times requiring large views, and new thoughts, new places. Introspective reflections that might otherwise be liable to stall are helped along by the flow of the landscape. The mind may be reluctant to think properly when thinking is all it is supposed to do; the task can be as paralysing as having to tell a joke or mimic an accent on demand. Thinking improves when parts of the mind are given other tasks—charged with listening to music, for example, or following a line of trees. The music or the view distracts for a time that nervous, censorious, practical part of the mind which is inclined to shut down when it notices something difficult emerging in con-

Edward Hopper, *Compartment C, Car 293*, 1938

sciousness, and which runs scared of memories, longings and introspective or original ideas, preferring instead the administrative and the impersonal.

Of all modes of transport, the train is perhaps the best aid to thought. The views have none of the potential monotony of those on a ship or a plane, moving quickly enough for us not to get exasperated but slowly enough to allow us to identify objects. They offer us brief, inspiring glimpses into private domains, letting us see a woman at the precise moment when she takes a cup from a shelf in her kitchen, then carrying us on to a patio where a man is sleeping and then to a park where a child is catching a ball thrown by a figure we cannot see.

On a journey across flat country, I think with a rare lack of inhibition about the death of my father, about an essay I am writing on Stendhal and about a mistrust that has arisen between two friends. Every time my mind goes blank, having hit on a difficult idea, the flow of consciousness is assisted by the possibility of looking out the window, locking on to object and following it for a few seconds, until a new coil of thought is ready to form and can unravel without pressure.

At the end of hours of train-dreaming, we may feel we have been returned to ourselves—that is, brought back into contact with emotions and ideas of importance to us. It is not necessarily at home that we best encounter our true selves. The furniture insists that we cannot change because it does not; the domestic setting keeps us tethered to the person we are in ordinary life, who may not be who we essentially are.

Hotel rooms offer us a similar opportunity to escape our habits of mind. Lying in bed in a hotel, the room quiet except for the occasional swooshing of an elevator in the innards of the building, we can draw a line under what preceded our arrival; we can overfly great and ignored stretches of our experience and reflect upon our lives from a height we could not have reached in the midst of our everyday business. We may be subtly assisted in this endeavour by the unfamiliar world around us—by the small wrapped soaps on the edge of the basin, by the gallery of miniature bottles in the minibar, by the room-service menu with its promises of all-night dining and by the view onto an unknown city stirring silently twenty-five floors below us.

Hotel note pads can be the recipients of unexpectedly intense, revelatory thoughts, taken down in the early hours while the breakfast menu ('to be hung outside before 3:00 A.M.') lies unattended on the floor, along with a card announcing the next day's weather and the management's best wishes for a peaceful night.

8.

The value we ascribe to the process of travelling, to wandering without reference to a destination, connects us, the critic Raymond Williams once suggested, to a broad shift in sensibilities dating back to some two hundred years ago, whereby the outsider came to seem morally superior to the insider:

From the late eighteenth century onwards, it is no longer from the practice of community but from being a wanderer that the instinct of fellow-feeling is derived. Thus an essential isolation and silence and loneliness become the carriers of nature and community against the rigours, the cold abstinence, the selfish ease of ordinary society.

Raymond Williams, *The Country and the City*

Edward Hopper, *Hotel Room*, 1931

MOTIVES

III

On the Exotic

Place |
Amsterdam

Guide | Gustave Flaubert

1.

On disembarking at Amsterdam's Schipol Airport, I am struck, only a few steps inside the terminal, by the appearance of a sign hanging from the ceiling, which announces the way to the arrivals hall, the exit and the transfer desks. It is a bright-yellow sign, one metre high and two metres across, simple in design, a plastic fascia in an illuminated aluminium box suspended on steel struts from a ceiling webbed with cables and air-conditioning ducts. Despite its simplicity, even its mundanity, the sign delights me, a delight for which the adjective *exotic*, though unusual, seems apt. The exoticism is located in particular areas: in the double *a* of *Aankomst*, in the neighbourliness of the *u* and the *i* in *Uitgang*, in the use of English subtitles, in the word for 'desk', *balies*, and in the choice of practical, modernist fonts, Frutiger or Univers.

If the sign provokes in me genuine pleasure, it is in part because it offers the first conclusive evidence of my having arrived elsewhere. It is a symbol of being abroad. Although it may not seem distinctive to the casual eye, such a sign would never exist in precisely this form in my own country. There it would be less yellow, the typeface would be softer and more nostalgic, there would—out of greater indifference to the confusion of foreigners—be no subtitles, and the language would contain no double *a*s, a repetition in which I sense, confusedly, the presence of another history and mind-set.

A plug socket, a bathroom tap, a jam jar or an airport sign may tell us more than its designer intended; it may speak of the nation that made it. And the nation that made the sign at Schipol Airport seems very far from my own. A bold archaeologist of national character might trace the influence of the lettering back to the de Stijl movement of the early twentieth century, the prominence of the English

subtitles to the Dutch openness towards foreign influences and the foundation of the East India Company in 1602, and the overall simplicity of the sign to the Calvinist aesthetic that became a part of Holland's identity during the war between the United Provinces and Spain in the sixteenth century.

That a sign could evolve so differently in two places is evidence of a simple but pleasing idea: countries are diverse, and practices variable across borders. Yet difference alone would not be enough to elicit pleasure, or not for long. The difference has to seem like an improvement on what my own country is capable of. If I call the Schipol sign exotic, it is because it succeeds in suggesting, vaguely but intensely, that the country that made it and that lies beyond the *uitgang* may in critical ways prove more congenial than my own to my temperament and concerns. The sign is a promise of happiness.

2.

The word *exotic* has traditionally been attached to more colourful things than Dutch signs, among them snake charmers, harems, minarets, camels, souks and mint tea poured from a great height into a tray of small glasses by a moustachioed servant.

In the first half of the nineteenth century, the term became synonymous with the Middle East. When Victor Hugo published his cycle of poems *Les Orientales* in 1829, he could declare in the preface, 'We are all much more concerned with the Orient than ever before. The Orient has become a subject of general preoccupation, to which the author of this book has deferred.'

Hugo's poems featured the staples of European Orientalist literature: pirates, pashas, sultans, spices, moustaches and dervishes. Characters drank mint tea from small glasses. His work found an eager audience, as did the *Arabian Nights*, the Oriental novels of Walter Scott and Byron's *The Giaour.* In January 1832, Eugène Delacroix set off for North Africa to capture the exoticism of the Orient in painting. Within three months of arriving in Tangier, he was wearing local dress and signing himself off in letters to his brother as 'your African'.

Even European public places were becoming more Oriental in appearance. On the fourteenth of September 1833, a crowd lined the banks of the Seine near Rouen and cheered as a French Navy boat christened the *Louxor* sailed upstream to Paris on its way from Alexandria, bearing, in a specially constructed hold, the giant obelisk lifted from the temple complex at Thebes, destined for a traffic island on the Place de la Concorde.

One of the spectators was a moody twelve-year-old boy named Gustave Flaubert, whose greatest wish was to leave Rouen, become a camel driver in Egypt and lose his virginity in a harem, to an olive-skinned woman with a trace of down on her upper lip.

The youngster held Rouen—indeed, the whole of France—in profound contempt. As he put it to his school friend Ernest Chevalier, he felt nothing but disdain for this 'good civilisation' that prided itself on having produced 'railways, poisons, cream tarts, royalty and the guillotine'. His life was 'sterile, banal and laborious'. 'Often I feel like blowing the heads off passersby,' he told his diary. 'I am bored, I am bored, I am bored.' He returned repeatedly to the theme of how boring it was to live in France, and especially in Rouen. 'Today my boredom was terrible,' he reported at the end of one bad Sunday. 'How beautiful are the provinces and how chic are the comfortably off who live there! Their talk is ... of taxes and road improvements. The *neighbour* is a wonderful institution. To be given

Eugène Delacroix, *Doors and Bay-Windows in an Arab House,* 1832

its full social due, his position should always be written in capital letters: NEIGHBOUR.'

It was as a source of relief from the prosperous pettiness and civic-mindedness of his surroundings that Flaubert contemplated the Orient. References to the Middle East pervaded his early writings and correspondence. In 'Rage et Impuissance', a story written in 1836, when Flaubert was fifteen (he was at school and fantasised about killing the mayor of Rouen), the author projected his Eastern fantasies onto his central character, M. Ohmlin, who longed for 'the Orient with her burning sun, her blue skies, her golden minarets...her caravans through the sands—the Orient!... The tanned, olive skin of Asiatic women!'

In 1839 (Flaubert was reading Rabelais and wanted to fart loudly enough for all Rouen to hear), he wrote another story, 'Les Memoires d'un fou', whose autobiographical hero looked back on a youth spent yearning for the Middle East: 'I dreamt of faraway journeys through the lands of the South; I saw the Orient, her vast sands and her palaces teeming with camels wearing brass bells.... I saw blue seas, a pure sky, silvery sand and women with tanned skin and fiery eyes who could whisper to me in the language of the Houris.'

Two years later (by which time Flaubert had left Rouen and was studying law in Paris, in deference to his father's wishes), he wrote another story, 'Novembre', whose hero had no time for railways, bourgeois civilisation or lawyers but instead identified with the traders of the East: 'Oh! To be riding now on the back of a camel! Ahead a red sky and brown sands, on the burning horizon the undulating landscape stretching out into infinity.... In the evening one puts up one's tent, waters the dromedaries and lights a fire to scare off the jackals that can be heard wailing far off in the desert; in the morning one fills the gourds at the oasis.'

In Flaubert's mind, the word *happiness* became interchangeable with the word *Orient*. In a moment of despair over his studies, his lack of romantic success, the expectations of his parents, the weather and the accompanying complaints of farmers (it had been raining for two weeks, and several cows had drowned in flooded fields near Rouen), Flaubert wrote to Chevalier, 'My life, which in my dreams is so beautiful, so poetic, so vast, so filled with love, will turn out to be like everyone else's: monotonous, sensible, stupid. I'll attend law school, be admitted to the bar and end up as a respectable assistant district attorney in a small provincial town such as Yvetot or Dieppe.... Poor madman, who dreamt of glory, love, laurels, journeys, the Orient.'

The people who lived along the coasts of North Africa, Saudi Arabia, Egypt, Palestine and Syria might have been surprised to learn that their lands had been grouped by a young Frenchman into a vague synonym for all that was good. 'Long live the sun, long live orange trees, palm trees, lotus flowers and cool pavilions paved in marble with wood-panelled chambers that talk of love!' he exclaimed. 'Will I never see necropolises where, towards evening, when the camels have come to rest by their wells, hyenas howl from beneath the mummies of kings?'

As it happened, he would, for when Gustave was twenty-four, his father died unexpectedly, leaving him a fortune that allowed him to sidestep the bourgeois career he had seemed destined for, with its attendant small talk about drowned cattle. He began at once to plan an Egyptian trip, assisted in the task by his friend Maxime Du Camp, a fellow student who shared his passion for the East and combined it with the practical turn of mind that was a necessary requirement for anyone wishing to undertake a journey there.

The two Oriental enthusiasts left Paris at the end of October 1849 and after a stormy sea crossing from Marseilles arrived in Alexandria in the middle of November. 'When we were two hours out from the coast of Egypt, I went up to the bow with the chief quartermaster and saw the seraglio of Abbas Pasha like a black dome on the blue of the Mediterranean,' Flaubert reported to his mother. 'The sun was beating down on it. I had my first sight of the Orient through, or rather in, a glowing light that was like melted silver on the sea. Soon the shore became distinguishable; the first thing we saw on land was a pair of camels led by their driver, and then, on the dock, some Arabs peacefully fishing. We landed amidst the most deafening uproar imaginable: Negroes, Negresses, camels, turbans, cudgellings to right and left, and earsplitting guttural cries. I gulped down a whole bellyful of colours, like a donkey filling himself with hay.'

3.

In Amsterdam, I took a room in a small hotel in the Jordaan district and after lunch in a café (*roggebrood met haring en uitjes*) went for a walk in the western parts of the city. In Flaubert's Alexandria, the exotic had collected around camels, Arabs peacefully fishing and guttural cries. Modern-day Amsterdam provided different but analogous examples: buildings with elongated pale-pink bricks stuck together with curiously white mortar (far more regular than English or North American brickwork, and exposed to view, unlike the bricks on French or German buildings); long rows of narrow apartment blocks from the early twentieth century, with large ground-floor windows; bicycles parked outside every house (recalling university towns); street furniture displaying a certain democratic scruffiness; an absence of ostentatious buildings; straight streets interspersed with small parks, suggesting the hand of planners with dreams of a socialist garden city. In one street lined with uniform apartment buildings,

I stopped by a red front door and felt an intense longing to spend the rest of my life there. Above me, on the second floor, I could see an apartment with three large windows and no curtains. The walls were painted white and decorated with a single large painting covered with small blue and red dots. There was an oaken desk against a wall, a large bookshelf and an armchair. I wanted the life that this space implied. I wanted a bicycle; I wanted to put my key in that red front door every evening. I wanted to stand by the curtainless window at dusk, looking out at the identical apartment opposite, and then snack my way through an *erwentsoep met roggebrood en spek* before retiring to read in bed in a white room with white sheets.

Why be seduced by something as small as a front door in another country? Why fall in love with a place because it has trams and its people seldom have curtains in their homes? However absurd the intense reactions provoked by such small (and mute) foreign elements may seem, the pattern is at least familiar from our personal lives. There, too, we may find ourselves anchoring emotions of love on the way a person butters his or her bread, or recoiling at his or her taste in shoes. To condemn ourselves for these minute concerns is to ignore how rich in meaning details may be.

My love for the apartment building was based on what I perceived to be its modesty. The building was comfortable but not grand. It suggested a society attracted to a financial mean. There was an honesty in its design. Whereas front doorways in London are prone to ape the look of classical temples, in Amsterdam they accept their status, avoiding pillars and plaster in favor of neat, undecorated brick. The building was modern in the best sense, speaking of order, cleanliness and light.

In the more fugitive, trivial association of the word *exotic*, the charm of a foreign place arises from the simple idea of novelty and

change—from finding camels where at home there are horses, for example, or unadorned apartment buildings where at home there are pillared ones. But there may be a more profound pleasure as well: we may value foreign elements not only because they are new but because they seem to accord more faithfully with our identity and commitments than anything our homeland can provide.

And so it was with my enthusiasms in Amsterdam, which were connected to my dissatisfactions with my own country, including its lack of modernity and aesthetic simplicity, its resistance to urban life and its net-curtained mentality.

What we find exotic abroad may be what we hunger for in vain at home.

4.

To understand why Flaubert found Egypt exotic, it may hence be useful first to examine his feelings towards France. What would strike him as exotic—that is, both new and valuable—about Egypt was in many ways the obverse of what drove him to rage at home. And that was, baldly stated, the beliefs and behaviour of the French bourgeoisie, which since the fall of Napoleon had become the dominant force in society, determining the tenor of the press, politics, manners and public life. For Flaubert, the French bourgeoisie was a repository of the most extreme prudery, snobbery, smugness, racism and pomposity. 'It's strange how the most banal utterances [of the bourgeoisie] sometimes make me marvel,' he complained in stifled rage. 'There are gestures, sounds of people's voices, that I cannot get over, silly remarks that almost give me vertigo. . . . The bourgeois . . . is for me something unfathomable.' He nevertheless spent

Street in Amsterdam

thirty years trying to fathom it, most comprehensively in his *Dictionary of Received Ideas*, a satirical catalogue of the French bourgeoisie's more striking sheeplike prejudices.

The organisation of only a few of these dictionary entries by theme indicates the direction of his complaints against his homeland, the foundation upon which his admiration for Egypt would be built:

A SUSPICION OF ARTISTIC ENDEAVOUR

ABSINTHE—Exceptionally violent poison: one glass and you're a dead man. Journalists drink it while writing their articles. Has killed more soldiers than the Bedouins.

ARCHITECTS—All idiots; always forget to put staircases in houses.

INTOLERANCE FOR AND IGNORANCE OF OTHER COUNTRIES (AND THEIR ANIMALS):

ENGLISHWOMEN—Express surprise that they can have pretty children.

CAMEL—Has two humps, and the dromedary one; or else the camel has one and the dromedary two—nobody can ever remember which.

ELEPHANTS—Noted for their memory and worship of the sun.

FRENCH—The greatest people in the world.

HOTELS—Are first-rate only in Switzerland.

ITALIANS—All musical. All treacherous.

JOHN BULL—When you don't know an Englishman's name, call him John Bull.

KORAN—Book by Mohammed, which is all about women.

BLACKS—Express surprise that their saliva is white and that they can speak French.

BLACK WOMEN—Hotter than white women (see also BRUNETTES and BLONDES).

BLACK—Always followed by 'as ebony'.

OASIS—An inn in the desert.

HAREM WOMEN—All Oriental women are harem women.

PALM TREE—Lends local colour.

MACHISMO/EARNESTNESS:

FIST—To govern France, an iron fist is needed.

GUN—Always keep one in the countryside.

BEARD—Sign of strength. Too much beard causes baldness. Helps to protect ties. (Flaubert to Louise Colet, August 1846: 'What stops me from taking myself seriously, even though I'm essentially a serious person, is that I find myself extremely ridiculous—not in the sense of the small-scale ridiculousness of slapstick comedy, but rather in the sense of a ridiculousness that seems intrinsic to human life and that manifests itself in the simplest actions and most ordinary gestures. For example, I can never shave without starting to laugh; it seems so idiotic. But all of this is very difficult to explain.')

SENTIMENTALITY:

ANIMALS—'If only animals could speak! There are some that are more intelligent than humans.'

COMMUNION—One's First Communion: the greatest day of one's life.

INSPIRATION (POETIC)—Aroused by: the sight of the sea, love, women, etc.

ILLUSIONS—Pretend to have had a great many, and complain that you have lost them all.

RAILWAYS—Enthuse about them, saying, 'I, my dear sir, who am speaking to you now, was at X this morning. I took the train to Y, transacted my business there, and by Z o'clock was back here.'

PRETENSION:

BIBLE—Oldest book in the world.

BEDROOM—In an old castle: Henry IV always spent a night in it.

MUSHROOMS—Should be bought only at the market.

CRUSADES—Benefited Venetian trade.

DIDEROT—Always followed by d'Alembert.

MELON—Good topic for dinnertime conversation. Is it a vegetable or a fruit? The English eat it for dessert, which is astonishing.

STROLL—Always take one after dinner; it helps with digestion.

SNAKES—All poisonous.

OLD PEOPLE—When discussing a flood, thunderstorm, etc., they cannot remember ever having seen a worse one.

PRISSINESS/REPRESSED SEXUALITY:

BLONDES—Hotter than brunettes (see also BRUNETTES).

BRUNETTES—Hotter than blondes (see also BLONDES).

SEX—Word to avoid. Say instead, 'Intimacy occurred ...'.

5.

Given all this, it appears to be no coincidence, no mere accident of fashion, that it was specifically the Middle East that Flaubert was interested in. It was temperamentally a logical fit. What he loved in Egypt could be traced back to central facets of his personality. Egypt lent support to ideas and values that were part of his identity but for which his own society had little sympathy.

(1) THE EXOTICISM OF CHAOS

From the day he disembarked in Alexandria, Flaubert noticed and felt at home in the chaos, both visual and auditory, of Egyptian life: boatmen shouting, Nubian porters hawking, merchants bargaining, the sounds of chickens being killed, donkeys being whipped, camels groaning.

In the streets there were, he said, 'guttural intonations that sound like the cries of wild beasts, and laughter, and flowing white robes, and ivory teeth flashing between thick lips and flat Negro noses, and dusty feet and necklaces and bracelets. 'It is like being hurled while still asleep into the midst of a Beethoven symphony, with the brasses at their most earsplitting, the basses rumbling, and the flutes sighing away; each detail reaches out to grip you; it pinches you; and the more you concentrate on it, the less you grasp the whole ... it is such a bewildering chaos of colours that your poor imagination is dazzled as though by continuous fireworks as you go about staring at minarets thick with white storks, at tired slaves stretched out in the sun on house terraces, at the patterns of sycamore branches against walls, with camel bells ringing in your ears and great herds of black goats bleating in the streets amidst the horses and the donkeys and the peddlers.'

Flaubert's aesthetic was a rich one. He liked purple, gold and turquoise and thus welcomed the colours of Egyptian architecture. In his book *The Manners and Customs of the Modern Egyptians*, first published in 1833 and revised in 1842, the English traveller Edward Lane described the interiors typical of Egyptian merchants' houses:

'There are, besides the windows of lattice-work, others, of coloured glass, representing bunches of flowers, peacocks, and other gay and gaudy objects, or merely fanciful patterns.... On the plastered walls of some apartments are rude paintings of the temple of Mecca, or of the tomb of the Prophet, or of flowers and other objects, executed by native Muslim artists.... Sometimes the walls are beautifully ornamented with Arabic inscriptions of maxims in an embellished style.'

The baroque quality of Egypt extended to the language used by Egyptians in even the most ordinary situations. Flaubert recorded some examples: 'A while ago when I was looking at seeds in a shop, a woman to whom I had given something said, "Blessings on you, my sweet lord; God grant that you return safe and sound to your native land." ... When [Maxime Du Camp] asked a groom if he wasn't tired, the answer was, "The pleasure of being seen by you suffices." '

Why did the chaos, the richness, so touch Flaubert? Because of his belief that life was fundamentally chaotic and that aside from art, all attempts to create order implied a censorious and prudish denial of our condition. He expressed his feelings to his mistress Louise Colet, in a letter written during a trip to London in September 1851, only a few months after his return from Egypt: 'We've just come back from a walk in Highgate Cemetery. What a gross corruption of Egyptian and Etruscan architecture it all is! How neat and tidy it is! The people in there seem to have died wearing white gloves. I hate little gardens around graves, with well-raked flower beds and flowers in bloom. This antithesis has always seemed to me to have come out of a bad novel. When it comes to cemeteries, I like those that are

Bazaar of the Silk Mercers, Cairo, lithograph by Louis Haghe after a drawing by David Roberts

run-down, ravaged, in ruins, full of thorns or tall weeds, and where a cow escaped from a neighbouring field has come to graze quietly. Admit that this is better than some policeman in uniform! How stupid order is!'

(II) THE EXOTICISM OF SHITTING DONKEYS

'Yesterday we were at a café that is one of the best in Cairo,' wrote Flaubert a few months after his arrival in the capital, 'and where there were at the same time as ourselves, inside, a donkey shitting and a gentleman pissing in a corner. No one finds such things odd; no one says anything.' And in Flaubert's eyes, they were right not to.

Central to Flaubert's philosophy was the belief that humans were not simply spiritual creatures but also pissing and shitting ones, and that we should integrate the ramifications of this blunt idea into our view of the world. 'I can't believe that man's body, composed as it is of mud and shit and equipped with instincts lower than those of the pig or the crab louse, contains anything pure and immaterial,' he told Ernest Chevalier. Which was not to say that we humans were without any higher dimensions; it was just that the prudery and self-righteousness of the age aroused in Flaubert a desire to remind others of mankind's impurities, occasionally by taking the side of café urinators (or even the Marquis de Sade, advocate of buggery, incest, rape and underage sex: 'I've just read a biographical article about de Sade by [the famous critic] Janin,' he informed Chevalier, 'which filled me with revulsion—revulsion against Janin, needless to say, who held forth on behalf of morality, philanthropy, deflowered virgins...').

Engraving from Edward Lane's *An Account of the Manners and Customs of the Modern Egyptians* (1842): *Private Houses in Cairo*

Flaubert found and welcomed in Egyptian culture a readiness to accept life's duality: shit-mind, life-death, sexuality-purity, madness-sanity. People belched to their hearts' content in restaurants. A boy of six or seven, passing Flaubert in a Cairo street, cried out in greeting, 'I wish you all kinds of prosperity, especially a long prick.' Edward Lane also noted this duality, though he reacted to it more in the manner of Janin than of Flaubert: 'The most immodest freedom of conversation is indulged in by persons of both sexes, and of every station of life, in Egypt; even by the most virtuous and respectable women. From persons of the best education, expressions are often heard so obscene as only to be fit for a low brothel; and things are named, and subjects talked of, by the most genteel women, without any idea of their being indecorous, in the hearing of men, that many prostitutes in our country would probably abstain from mentioning.'

(III) THE EXOTICISM OF CAMELS

'One of the finest things is the camel,' wrote Flaubert from Cairo. 'I never tire of watching this strange beast that lurches like a donkey and sways its neck like a swan. Its cry is something that I wear myself out trying to imitate—I hope to bring it back with me, but it's hard to reproduce: a rattle with a kind of tremulous gargling as an accompaniment.' Writing to a family friend a few months after he left Egypt, he listed the things that had most impressed him in that country: the pyramids, the temple at Karnak, the Valley of the Kings, some dancers in Cairo, a painter named Hassan el Bilbeis. 'But my real passion is the camel (please don't think I'm joking): nothing has a more singular grace than this melancholic animal. You have to see a group of them in the desert when they advance in single file across the horizon, like soldiers; their necks stick out like those of ostriches, and they keep going, going. . . .'

Why did Flaubert so admire the camel? Because he identified with its stoicism and ungainliness. He was touched by its sad expression and its combination of awkwardness and fatalistic resilience. The people of Egypt seemed to share some of the camel's qualities, exhibiting a silent strength and humility that contrasted with the bourgeois arrogance of Flaubert's own Norman neighbours.

Flaubert had since childhood resented the optimism of his country—a resentment he would express in *Madame Bovary*, through his description of the cruel scientific faith of the most detestable character, the pharmacist Homais—and himself had a predictably darker outlook: 'At the end of the day, shit. With that mighty word, you can console yourself for all human miseries, so I enjoy repeating it: shit, shit.' It was a philosophy reflected in the sad, noble yet slightly mischievous eyes of the Egyptian camel.

6.

In Amsterdam, on the corner of Tweede Helmers Straat and Eerste Constantijn Huygens Straat, I notice a woman in her late twenties pushing a bicycle along the pavement. Her auburn hair is drawn into a bun, she is wearing a long grey coat, an orange pullover, flat brown shoes and a pair of practical-looking glasses. It seems that this is her part of town, for she walks confidently and without curiosity. In a basket attached to the handlebars of her bicycle is a loaf of bread and a carton on which is written '*Goodappeltje.*' She sees nothing peculiar in the proximity of that *t* and *j*, stuck together without a vowel, on her apple-juice carton. There is nothing exotic for her in pushing a bicycle to the shops, or in the shape of those tall apartment blocks with their hooks on the top floor for hoisting furniture.

Desire elicits a need to understand. Where is she going? What are her thoughts? Who are her friends? On the riverboat that carried him and Du Camp to Marseilles, where they were to catch the steamer for Alexandria, Flaubert was overcome by similar questions about another woman. While other passengers gazed absentmindedly at the scenery, Flaubert fixed his eyes on a woman on deck. She was, he wrote in his Egyptian travel journal, 'a young and slender creature wearing a long green veil over her straw hat. Under her silk jacket, she had on a short frock coat with a velvet collar and pockets on either side in which she had put her hands. Two rows of buttons ran down her front, holding her in tightly and tracing the outline of her hips, from which flowed the numerous pleats of her dress, which rubbed against her knees in the wind. She wore tight black gloves and spent most of the journey leaning against the railing and looking out at the banks of the river.... I'm obsessed with inventing stories for people I come across. An overwhelming curiosity makes me ask myself what their lives might be like. I want to know what they do, where they're from, their names, what they're thinking about at that moment, what they regret, what they hope for, whom they've loved, what they dream of... and if they happen to be women (especially youngish ones), then the urge becomes intense. How quickly you would want to see that one naked, admit it, and naked through to her heart. How you try to learn where she's coming from, where she's going, why she's here and not elsewhere! While letting your eyes wander all over her, you imagine love affairs for her, you ascribe deep feelings to her. You think of what her bedroom could look like, and a thousand things besides... right down to the battered slippers into which she must slip her feet when she gets out of bed.'

Eugène Delacroix, *Women of Algiers in Their Apartment*, 1834

To the appeal that an attractive person might possess in one's own country is added, in an exotic land, an attraction deriving from his or her location. If it is true that love is the pursuit in another of qualities we lack in ourselves, then in our love of someone from another country, one ambition may be to weld ourselves more closely to values missing from our own culture.

In his Moroccan paintings, Delacroix appeared to suggest how desire for a place might fuel desire for the people within it. Of the subjects of his *Women of Algiers in Their Apartment* (1849), for example, the viewer might long to know, as Flaubert longed to know of the women he passed, 'their names, what they're thinking about at that moment, what they regret, what they hope for, whom they've loved, what they dream of...'.

Flaubert's legendary sexual experience in Egypt was commercial, but not unfeeling. It took place in the small town of Esna, on the western bank of the Nile, some fifty kilometres south of Luxor. Flaubert and Du Camp stopped in Esna for the night and were introduced to a famous courtesan, who also had a reputation as an *almeh*, or learned woman. The word *prostitute* does not capture the dignity of Kuchuk Hanem's role. Flaubert desired her at first sight: 'Her skin, particularly on her body, is slightly coffee-coloured. When she bends, her flesh ripples into bronze ridges. Her eyes are dark and enormous. Her eyebrows are black, her nostrils open and wide; broad shoulders, full, apple-shaped breasts ... black hair that is wavy, unruly, pulled straight back on each side from a centre part beginning at the forehead.... She has one upper incisor, on the right, that is starting to go bad.'

She invited Flaubert back to her modest house. It was an unusually cold night, with a clear sky. In his notebook, the Frenchman recorded: 'We went to bed ... she fell asleep with her hand in mine.

She snored. The lamp, shining feebly, cast a triangular gleam, the colour of pale metal, on her beautiful forehead; the rest of her face was in shadow. Her little dog slept on my silk jacket on the divan. Since she had complained of a cough, I put my pelisse over her blanket.... I gave myself over to intense reveries, full of reminiscences. The feeling of her stomach against my buttocks. Her mound, warmer than her stomach, heated me like a hot iron ... we told each other a great many things through touch. As she slept, she kept contracting her hands and thighs mechanically, as if involuntarily shuddering.... How flattering it would be to one's pride if at the moment of leaving one could be sure of having left some memory behind, so that she would think of one more than of the others who have been there, and keep one in her heart!'

Dreams of Kuchuk Hanem accompanied Flaubert down the Nile. On their way back from Philae and Aswan, he and Du Camp stopped off at Esna to visit her once more. Their second meeting made Flaubert even more melancholy: 'Infinite sadness ... this is the end; I'll not see her again, and gradually her face will fade from my memory.' It never did.

7.

We are taught to be suspicious of the exotic reveries of European men who spend nights with locals while travelling through Oriental lands. Was Flaubert's enthusiasm for Egypt anything more than a fantasy of an alternative to the homeland he resented, a childhood idealisation of the 'Orient' extended into adulthood?

However vague his vision of Egypt may have been at the beginning of his journey, Flaubert could, after a stay of nine months, claim a genuine understanding of the country. Within three days of arriving in Alexandria, he began to study its language and history.

He hired a teacher to talk him through Muslim customs, at the rate of three francs an hour, four hours a day. After two months, he sketched plans for a book to be entitled *Muslim Customs* (never written), which was to contain chapters on birth, circumcision, marriage, the pilgrimage to Mecca, death rites and the Last Judgement. He memorised passages of the Koran from Guillaume Pauthier's *Les Livres sacres de l'Orient* and read the major European works on Egypt, among them C. F. Volney's *Voyage en Egypte et en Syrie* and Chardin's *Voyages en Perse et autres lieux de l'Orient.* In Cairo, he had conversations with the Copt bishop and explored the Armenian, Greek and Sunnite communities. His dark skin tone, beard and moustache and command of the language often caused him to be mistaken for a native. He wore a large white cotton Nubian shirt trimmed with red pompons and shaved his head, leaving only a single lock at the occiput, 'by which Mohammed lifts one up on Judgement Day.' He even acquired a local name, as he explained to his mother: 'Since the Egyptians have great difficulty pronouncing French names, they invent their own for us Franks. Can you guess? Abu Chanab, which means "Father of the Moustache". That word *abu,* "father," is applied to anyone important in whatever field is being spoken about; thus merchants selling various commodities are referred to as Father of the Shoes, Father of the Glue, Father of the Mustard, etc.'

For Flaubert, properly understanding Egypt meant discovering that it was not, after all, everything it had seemed to be from the distance of Rouen. Naturally, there were disappointments. To judge by the account of their Egyptian journey written many years after the fact by an embittered Maxime Du Camp—who was patently keen to

Gustave Flaubert in Cairo, 1850, in the garden of his hotel

take aim at an author more celebrated than he, to whom he was, moreover, no longer so close—Flaubert was, implausibly, as bored on the Nile as he had been in Rouen: 'Flaubert shared none of my exultation; he was quiet and withdrawn. He was averse to movement and action. He would have liked to travel, if he could have done, stretched out on a sofa and not stirring, watching landscapes, ruins and cities pass before him like the screen of a panorama mechanically unwinding. From our very first days in Cairo I had been aware of his lassitude and boredom: this journey, which he had so cherished as a dream and whose realisation had seemed to him so impossible, did not satisfy him. I was very direct; I said to him, "If you wish to return to France, I will send my servant to accompany you." He replied, "No, I began it, and I'll go through with it; you take care of the itineraries, and I'll fit in—it's the same to me whether I go right or left." The temples seemed to him always alike, the mosques and the landscapes all the same. I am not sure that when gazing at the island of Elephantine he did not sigh for the meadows of Sotteville, or long for the Seine when he saw the Nile.'

Du Camp's charge was not altogether unfounded. In a moment of dejection near Aswan, Flaubert had written in his diary, 'The Egyptian temples bore me profoundly. Are they going to become like the churches in Brittany, the waterfalls in the Pyrenees? O necessity! To do what you are supposed to do, to be always, according to the circumstances (and despite the aversion of the moment), what a young man, or a tourist, or an artist, or a son, or a citizen, etc., is supposed to be!' Camped at Philae a few days later, he continued: 'I don't stir from the island and am depressed. What is it, O Lord, this permanent lassitude that I drag about with me? ... Deianira's tunic was no less completely welded to Hercules' back than boredom to my life! It eats into it more slowly, that's all.'

And desperately though Flaubert had hoped to escape what he deemed to be the extraordinary idiocy of the modern European bourgeoisie, he found that it followed him everywhere: 'Stupidity is an immovable object: you can't try to attack it without being broken by it.... In Alexandria, a certain Thompson, of Sunderland, has inscribed his name in letters six feet high on Pompey's Pillar. You can read it from a quarter of a mile away. You can't see the pillar without seeing Thompson's name and consequently thinking of Thompson. This cretin has thus become part of the monument and has perpetuated himself along with it. But what am I saying? He has in fact *overwhelmed* it with the splendour of his gigantic lettering.... All imbeciles are more or less Thompsons from Sunderland. How many of them one comes across in life, in the most beautiful places and in front of the finest views! When travelling, one meets them often ... but as they go by quickly, one can laugh at them. It's not like in ordinary life, where they end up making one fierce.'

Yet none of this meant that Flaubert's original attraction to Egypt had been misconceived. He simply replaced an absurdly idealised image with a more realistic but nevertheless still profoundly admiring one, he exchanged a youthful crush for a knowledgeable love. Irritated by Du Camp's caricature of him as the disappointed tourist, he told Alfred le Poitevin, 'A bourgeois would say, "If you go, you'll be greatly disillusioned." But I have rarely experienced disillusion, having had few illusions. What a stupid platitude, always to glorify the lie and say that poetry lives on illusions!'

Writing to his mother, he accurately defined what his journey had taught him: 'You ask whether the Orient is all I imagined it to be. Yes, it is—and more than that, it extends far beyond the narrow idea I had of it. I have found, clearly delineated, everything that was hazy in my mind.'

8.

When the time came for him and Du Camp to leave Egypt, Flaubert was distraught. 'When will I see a palm tree again? When will I climb on a dromedary again?' he asked, and throughout the rest of his life he was to return constantly to the country in his mind. A few days before his death, in 1880, he would tell his niece Caroline, 'For the past two weeks I have been gripped by the desire to see a palm tree standing out against the blue sky, and to hear a stork clacking its beak at the top of a minaret.'

Flaubert's lifelong relationship with Egypt seems like an invitation to deepen and respect our own attraction to certain countries. From his adolescence onwards, Flaubert insisted that he was not French. His hatred of his nation and its people was so profound as to make a mockery of his civil status. Hence he proposed a new method for ascribing nationality: not according to the country of a person's birth or ancestral origins, but instead according to the places to which he or she was attracted. (It was only logical for him to extend this more flexible concept of identity to gender and species, and consequently to declare on occasion that contrary to appearances, he was in truth a woman, a camel and a bear: 'I want to buy myself a beautiful bear—a painting of one, that is—frame it and hang it in my bedroom, with *Portrait of Gustave Flaubert* written beneath it, to suggest my moral disposition and social habits,' he announced.)

Flaubert's first development of the idea that he belonged somewhere other than France came in a letter he wrote as a schoolboy, on his return from a holiday in Corsica: 'I'm disgusted to be back in this damned country where one sees the sun in the sky about as often as a diamond in a pig's arse. I don't give a shit for Normandy and *la belle France*. . . . I think I must have been transplanted by the winds to this land of mud; surely I was born elsewhere—I've always had what seem to be memories or intuitions of perfumed shores and blue seas. I was born to be the emperor of Cochin-China, to smoke hundred-foot-long pipes, to have six thousand wives and fourteen hundred catamites, scimitars to slice off heads I don't like the looks of, Numidian horses, marble pools.'

The alternative to *la belle France* may have been impractical, but the underlying principle of the letter—the belief that he had been 'transplanted by the winds'—was to find repeated and more reasoned expression in his maturity. On his return from Egypt, Flaubert attempted to explain his theory of national identity (though not of species or gender) to Louise Colet ('my sultan'): 'As to the idea of a native country, that is to say a certain bit of ground traced out on a map and separated from other bits by a red or blue line: no. For me, my native country is the country I love, meaning the one that makes me dream, that makes me feel well. I am as much Chinese as I am French, and I cannot rejoice about our victories over the Arabs because I am saddened by their defeats. I love those harsh, enduring, hardy people, the last of the primitives, who at midday lie down in the shade under the bellies of their camels and, while smoking their chibouks, poke fun at our good civilisation, which quivers with rage over it.'

Louise replied that she found it absurd to think of Flaubert as being either Chinese or Arab, a retort that provoked the novelist, in a letter written a few days later, to return to his charge with greater emphasis and irritation: 'I'm no more modern than ancient, no more French than Chinese, and the idea of a native country—that is to say, the imperative to live on one bit of ground marked red or blue on the map and to hate the other bits in green or black—has always seemed to me narrow-minded, blinkered and profoundly stupid. I am a soul brother to everything that lives, to the giraffe and to the crocodile as much as to man.'

We are all of us, without ever having any say in the matter, scattered at birth by the wind onto various countries, but like Flaubert, we are in adulthood granted the freedom imaginatively to re-create our identity in line with our true allegiances. When we grow weary of our official nationality (from Flaubert's *Dictionary of Received Ideas*: 'FRENCH—"How proud one is to be French when one looks at the Colonne Vendôme!" '), we may withdraw to those parts of ourselves that are more Bedouin than Norman, that delight in riding on a camel through a khamsin, in sitting in a café beside a shitting donkey and in engaging in what Edward Lane called 'licentious conversation'.

When asked where he came from, Socrates said not 'From Athens' but 'From the world.' Flaubert was from Rouen (in his youthful account, a place drowning in 'merde', whose good citizens 'jerk themselves silly' on Sundays out of boredom), and yet Abu Chanab, the Father of the Moustache, might have answered, perhaps a little from Egypt, too.

IV

On Curiosity

Place	*Madrid*
Guide	*Alexander von Humboldt*

1.

In the springtime I was invited to Madrid to attend a three-day conference that was scheduled to end on a Friday afternoon. Because I had never visited the city before and had been told on several occasions of its many attractions (which were apparently not limited to museums), I decided to extend my stay by a few days. My hosts had booked me a hotel on a wide, tree-lined avenue in the southeastern part of the city. My room overlooked a courtyard in which a short man with a certain resemblance to Philip II occasionally stood and smoked a cigarette while tapping his foot on the steel door of what I supposed was a cellar. On the Friday evening, I retired early to my room. I had not revealed to my hosts that I would be staying the weekend, for fear of forcing them into a halfhearted hospitality from which neither side would benefit. But my decision also meant that I had to go without dinner, for I realised on walking back to the hotel that I was too shy to venture alone into any of the neighbourhood restaurants, all dark, wood-panelled places, many with a ham hanging from the ceiling, where I risked becoming an object of curiosity and pity. So I ate a packet of paprika-flavoured crisps from the minibar and, after watching the news on satellite television, fell asleep.

When I awoke the next morning, it was to an intense lethargy, as though my veins had become silted up with fine sugar or sand. Sunlight shone through the pink-and-grey plastic-coated curtains, and traffic could be heard along the avenue. On the desk lay several magazines provided by the hotel, offering information about the city, and two guidebooks that I had brought from home. In their different ways, they conspired to suggest that an exciting and multifarious phenomenon called Madrid was waiting to be discovered outside, promising an embarrassment of monuments, churches, museums, fountains, plazas and shopping streets. And yet the prospect of those enticements, about which I had heard so much and which I knew I was privileged to be able to see, merely provoked in me a combination of listlessness and self-disgust at the contrast between my own indolence and what I imagined would have been the eagerness of more normal visitors. My overwhelming wish was to remain in bed and, if possible, catch an early flight home.

2.

In the summer of 1799, a twenty-nine-year-old German by the name of Alexander von Humboldt set sail from the Spanish port of La Coruña, bound for the South American continent on a voyage of exploration.

'From my earliest days I had felt the urge to travel to distant lands seldom visited by Europeans,' he would later recall. 'The study of maps and the perusal of travel books aroused in me a secret fascination that was at times almost irresistible.' The young German was ideally suited to follow up on his fascination. Along with great physical stamina, he had expertise in biology, geology, chemistry, physics and history. As a student at the University of Göttingen, he had befriended Georg Forster, the naturalist who had accompanied Captain Cook on his second voyage, and mastered the art of classifying plant and animal species. Since finishing his studies, Humboldt had been looking for opportunities to travel to someplace remote and unknown. Plans to go to Egypt and Mecca had fallen through at the last moment, but in the spring of 1799, Humboldt had had the good fortune to meet King Charles IV of Spain and had persuaded him to underwrite his exploration of South America.

Humboldt was to be away from Europe for five years. On his return, he settled in Paris and over the next twenty years published a thirty-volume account of his travels, entitled *Journey to the Equinoctial Regions of the New Continent*. The length of the work was an accurate measure of Humboldt's achievements. Surveying these, Ralph Waldo Emerson was to write, 'Humboldt was one of those wonders of the world, like Aristotle, like Julius Caesar, like the Admirable Crichton, who appear from time to time as if to show us the possibilities of the human mind, the force and range of the faculties—a universal man.'

Much about South America was still unknown to Europe when Humboldt set sail from La Coruña: Vespucci and Bougainville had travelled around the shores of the continent, and La Condamine and Bouguer had surveyed the streams and mountains of the Amazon and of Peru, but there were still no accurate maps of the region, and little information had been gathered on its geology, botany and indigenous peoples. Humboldt transformed the state of knowledge. He travelled fifteen thousand kilometres around the northern coastlines and interior, on the way collecting some sixteen hundred plants and identifying six hundred new species. He redrew the map of South America based on readings supplied by accurate chronometers and sextants. He researched the Earth's magnetism and was the first to discover that magnetic intensity declined the further one got from the poles. He gave the first account of the rubber and cinchona trees. He mapped the streams connecting the Orinoco and Negro river systems. He measured the effects of air pressure and altitude on vegetation. He studied the kinship rituals of the people of the Amazon Basin and inferred connections between geography and cultural characteristics. He compared the

Eduard Ender, *Alexander von Humboldt and Aimé Bonpland in Venezuela, c.* 1850

salinity of water from the Pacific and the Atlantic and conceived the idea of sea currents, recognising that the temperature of the sea owed more to drifts than to latitude.

Humboldt's early biographer, F. A. Schwarzenberg, subtitled his life of Humboldt *What May Be Accomplished in a Lifetime*. He summarised the areas of his subject's extraordinary curiosity as follows: '1) The knowledge of the Earth and its inhabitants. 2) The discovery of the higher laws of nature, which govern the universe, men, animals, plants and minerals. 3) The discovery of new forms of life. 4) The discovery of territories hitherto but imperfectly known, and their various productions. 5) The acquaintance with new species of the human race—their manners, their language and the historical traces of their culture.'

What may be accomplished in a lifetime—and seldom or never is.

3.

It was a maid who was ultimately responsible for my own voyage of exploration around Madrid. Three times she burst into my room with a broom and basket of cleaning fluids and, at the sight of a huddled shape under the sheets, exclaimed with theatrical alarm '*Hola, perdone!*' before leaving again, taking care to let her utensils collide loudly with the door as she slammed it. Because I did not wish to encounter this apparition a fourth time, I dressed, ordered a hot chocolate and a plate of batter sticks in the hotel bar and made my way to a part of town identified by one of my guidebooks as 'Old Madrid':

When Felipe II chose Madrid as his capital in 1561, it was a small Castilian town with a population of barely twenty thousand. In the following years, it was to grow into the nerve centre of a mighty empire. Narrow streets with houses and medieval churches began to grow up behind the old Moorish fortress, which was later replaced by a Gothic palace and eventually by the present-day Bourbon palace, the Palacio Real. The sixteenth-century city is known as the 'Madrid de los Austrias' after the Habsburg dynasty. At this time, monasteries were endowed and churches and palaces were built. In the seventeenth century, the Plaza Mayor was added and the Puerta del Sol became the spiritual and geographical heart of Spain.

I stood on the corner of the Calle de Carretas and the Puerta del Sol, an undistinguished half-moon-shaped junction in the middle of which Carlos III (1759–1788) sat astride a horse. It was a sunny day, and crowds of tourists were stopping to take photographs and listen to guides. And I wondered, with mounting anxiety, What am I supposed to do here? What am I supposed to think?

4.

Humboldt was never pursued by such questions. Everywhere he went, his mission was unambiguous: to discover facts and to carry out experiments towards that end.

Already on the ship carrying him to South America, he had begun his factual researches. He measured the temperature of the seawater every two hours from Spain to the ship's destination, Cumaná, on the coast of New Granada (part of modern Venezuela). He took readings with his sextant and recorded the different marine species that he saw or found in the net he had hung from the stern. And once he landed in Venezuela, he threw himself into an exhaustive study of the vegetation around Cumaná. The hills of calcareous rock on which the town stood were dotted with cacti and opuntia, their trunks branching out like candelabras coated with lichen. One afternoon, Humboldt measured a cactus (*Tuna macho*) and noted its circumference: 1.54 metres. He spent three weeks cataloguing many more plants on the coast, then ventured inland into the jungle-covered New Andalusia mountain range. He took with him a mule bearing a trunk containing a sextant, a dipping needle, an instrument for calibrating magnetic variation, a thermometer and a Saussure's hygrometer, which measured humidity and was made of hair and whalebone. He put all of these to good use. In his journal he wrote, 'As we entered the jungle the barometer showed that we were gaining altitude. Here the tree trunks offered us an extraordinary view: a gramineous plant with verticillate branches climbed like a liana to a height of eight to ten feet, forming garlands that crossed our path and swung in the wind. At about three in the afternoon we stopped on a small plain known as Quetepe, some 190 toises above sea level. A few huts stood by a spring whose water was known by the Indians to be fresh and healthy. We found the water delicious. Its temperature was only 22.5°C, while the air was 28.7°C.'

5.

But in Madrid everything was already known; everything had already been measured. The northern side of the Plaza Mayor is 101 metres, 52 centimetres long. It was built by Juan Gómez de Mora in 1619. The temperature that day was 18.5 degrees centigrade, the wind from the West. The equestrian statue of Philip III in the middle of the Plaza Mayor is 5 metres, 43 centimetres high and was crafted by Giambologna and Pietro Tacca. The guidebook occasionally seemed impatient in presenting its facts. It sent me to the Pontificia de San Miguel, a grey building apparently designed to repel the casual glances of passersby, and declared:

The basilica by Bonavia is one of the rare Spanish churches to have been inspired by the eighteenth-century Italian baroque. Its convex facade, designed as an interplay of inward and outward curves, is adorned with fine statues. Above the doorway is a low relief of saints Justus and Pastor, to whom the basilica was previously dedicated. The interior is graceful and elegant with an oval cupola, intersecting ribbed vaulting, flowing cornices and abundant stuccowork.

If my level of curiosity was so far removed from Humboldt's (and my impulse to return to bed so strong), it was in part because of the range of advantages with which any traveller on a factual, as opposed to touristic, mission is blessed.

Facts have utility. Knowing the precise dimensions of the northern edge of the Plaza Mayor will be helpful to architects and students of the work of Juan Gómez de Mora. Accurate measurements of the barometric pressure on an April day in central Madrid will be of use to meteorologists. Humboldt's discovery that the circumference of the Cumanán cactus (*Tuna macho*) was 1.54 metres was of interest to biologists throughout Europe, who had not suspected that cacti could grow so large.

And with utility comes an (approving) audience. When Humboldt returned to Europe with his South American facts in August 1804, he was besieged and feted by interested parties. Six weeks after arriving in Paris, he read his first travel report to a packed audience at the Institut National. He informed his listeners of the respective water temperatures on the Pacific and Atlantic coasts of South America, and of the fifteen different species of monkeys he had recorded in the jungles. He opened twenty cases of fossil and mineral specimens, which a crowd pressed around the podium to see. The Bureau of Longitude Studies asked for a copy of his astronomic facts; the observatory requested his barometric measurements. He was invited to dinner by Chateaubriand and Madame de Staël and admitted to the elite Society of Arcueil, a scientific salon whose members included Laplace, Berthollet and Gay-Lussac. In Britain, his work was read by Charles Lyell and Joseph Hooker. Charles Darwin learnt large parts of his findings by heart.

As Humboldt walked around a cactus or stuck his thermometer into the Amazon, his own curiosity must have been guided by a sense of others' interests, and bolstered by it in the inevitable moments when lethargy or sickness threatened. It was fortunate for him that almost every existing fact about South America was wrong or questionable. When he sailed into Havana in November 1800, he discovered that even this most important strategic base for the Spanish Navy had not been placed correctly on the map. He unpacked his measuring instruments and worked out the correct geographical latitude. A grateful Spanish admiral invited him to dinner.

6.
Sitting in a café on the Plaza Provincia, I acknowledged the impossibility of new factual discoveries. My guidebook enforced the point with a lecture:

The neoclassical facade of the Iglesia de San Francisco el Grande is by Sabatini, but the building itself, a circular edifice with six radial chapels and a large dome 33 metres / 108 feet wide, is by Francisco Cabezas.

Anything I learnt would have to be justified by private benefit rather than by the interest of others. My discoveries would have to enliven me; they would have in some way to prove 'life-enhancing'.

The term was Nietzsche's. In the autumn of 1873, Friedrich Nietzsche composed an essay in which he distinguished between collecting facts like an explorer or academic and using already well known facts to the end of inner, psychological enrichment. Unusually for a university professor, he denigrated the former activity and praised the latter. Entitling his essay 'On the Uses and Disadvantages of History for Life', Nietzsche began with the extraordinary assertion that collecting facts in a quasi-scientific way was a sterile pursuit. The real challenge, he suggested, was to use facts to enhance 'life'. He quoted a sentence from Goethe: 'I hate everything that merely instructs me without augmenting or directly invigorating my activity.'

What would it mean to seek knowledge 'for life' in one's travels? Nietzsche offered suggestions. He imagined a person who, depressed about the state of German culture and the lack of any attempt being undertaken to improve it, went to an Italian city—Siena or Florence, say—and there discovered that the phenomenon broadly known as the Italian Renaissance had in fact been the work of only a few individuals, who with luck, perseverance and the right patrons had been able to shift the mood and values of a whole society. This tourist would learn to seek in other cultures 'that which in the past was able to expand the concept "man" and make it more beautiful', thus joining the ranks of those 'who, gaining strength through reflecting on past greatness, are inspired by the feeling that the life of man is a glorious thing.'

Nietzsche also proposed a second kind of tourism, whereby we may learn how our societies and identities have been formed by the past and so acquire a sense of continuity and belonging. The person practising this kind of tourism 'looks beyond his own individual transitory existence and feels himself to be the spirit of his house, his race, his city'. He can gaze at old buildings and feel 'the happiness of knowing that he is not wholly accidental and arbitrary but grown out of a past as its heir, flower and fruit, and that his existence is thus excused and indeed justified'.

To follow the Nietzschean line, the point of looking at an old building may be nothing more but then again nothing less than recognising that 'architectural styles are more flexible than they seem, as are the uses for which buildings are made'. We might look at the Palacio de Santa Cruz, for example (*'Constructed between 1629 and 1643, this building is one of the jewels of Habsburg architecture'*), and think, 'If it was possible then, why not something similar now?'

Instead of bringing back sixteen thousand new plant species, we might return from our journeys with a collection of small, unfeted but life-enhancing thoughts.

7.

There was another problem: the explorers who had come before and discovered facts had at the same time laid down distinctions between what was significant and what was not—distinctions that had, over time, hardened into almost immutable truths about where value lay in Madrid. The Plaza de la Villa had one star, the Palacio Real two stars, the Monasterio de las Descalzas Reales three stars, and the Plaza de Oriente no stars at all.

Such distinctions were not necessarily false, but their effect was pernicious. Where guidebooks praised a site, they pressured a visitor to match their authoritative enthusiasm, and where they were silent, pleasure or interest seemed unwarranted. Long before entering the three-star Monasterio de las Descalzas Reales, I knew the official enthusiasm that my own response would have to accord with: *'The most beautiful convent in Spain. A grand staircase decorated with frescoes leads to the upper cloister gallery, where each of the chapels is more sumptuous than its predecessor.'* The guidebook might have added, *'and where there must be something wrong with the traveller who cannot agree'.*

Humboldt did not suffer such intimidation. Few Europeans

before him had crossed the regions through which he travelled, and this absence offered him an imaginative freedom. He could unselfconsciously decide what interested him. He could create his own categories of value without either following or deliberately rebelling against the hierarchies of others. When he arrived at the San Fernando mission on the Río Negro, he was free to think that everything, or perhaps nothing, might be interesting. The needle of his curiosity followed its own magnetic north and, unsurprisingly to the future readers of his *Journey*, ended up pointing at plants. 'In San Fernando we were most struck by the *pihiguado* or *pirijao* plant, which gives the countryside its peculiar quality. Covered with thorns, its trunk reaches more than sixty feet high,' he reported at the top of his list of what was interesting in San Fernando. Next Humboldt measured the temperature (very hot), then noted that the missionaries lived in attractive houses that were matted with liana and surrounded by gardens.

I tried to imagine an uninhibited guide to Madrid; how I myself might have ranked the city's offerings according to a subjective hierarchy of interest. I had three-star levels of interest in the underrepresentation of vegetables in the Spanish diet (during the last proper meal I had eaten, only a few limp, bleached and apparently tinned spears of asparagus had appeared between a succession of meat dishes) and the long and noble-sounding surnames of ordinary citizens (the assistant in charge of organizing the conference, for example, had owned a train of surnames connected by *de* and *la*, an appellation that suggested an ancestral castle, faithful servants, an old well and a coat of arms, a projection in sharp contrast with the reality of her life: a dust-coated SEAT Ibiza and a studio flat near the airport). I was interested in the smallness of Spanish men's feet

Esmeralda, on the Orinoco, engraved by Paul Gauci after a drawing by Charles Bentley

and in the attitude towards modern architecture evident in many newer districts of the city—specifically, the fact that whether or not a building was attractive appeared to be less important than that it was obviously modern, even if this meant giving something a vile bronze facade (as though modernity were a longed-for substance that one needed in extra-strong doses to compensate for an earlier lack). All these matters would have appeared on my subjective list of interesting things in Madrid if my compass of curiosity had been allowed to settle according to its own logic, rather than being swayed by the unexpectedly powerful force field of a small green object by the name of *The Michelin Street Guide to Madrid,* which pointed its needle resolutely towards, among other targets, a brown-looking staircase in the echoing corridors of the Monasterio de las Descalzas Reales.

8.

In June 1802, Humboldt climbed up what was then thought to be the highest mountain in the world: the volcanic peak of Mount Chimborazo in Peru, 6,267 metres above sea level. 'We were constantly climbing through clouds,' he reported. 'In many places, the ridge was not wider than eight or ten inches. To our left was a precipice of snow whose frozen crust glistened like glass. On the right lay a fearful abyss, from eight hundred to a thousand feet deep, with huge masses of rocks projecting from it.' In spite of the danger, Humboldt found time to notice elements that would have passed most mortals by: 'A few rock lichens were seen above the snow lines, at a height of 16,920 feet. The last green moss we noticed about 2,600 feet lower down. A butterfly was captured by M. Bonpland [his travelling companion] at a height of 15,000 feet and a fly was seen 1,600 feet higher.'

Friedrich Georg Weitsch, *Alexander von Humboldt and Aimé Bonpland at the Foot of Chimborazo*, 1810

How does a person come to be interested in the exact height at which he or she sees a fly? How does he or she begin to care about a piece of moss growing on a volcanic ridge ten inches wide? In Humboldt's case, such curiosity was far from spontaneous: his concern had a long history. The fly and the moss attracted his attention because they were related to prior, larger and—to the layman—more understandable questions.

Curiosity might be pictured as being made up of chains of small questions extending outwards, sometimes over huge distances, from a central hub composed of a few blunt, large questions. In childhood we ask, 'Why is there good and evil?' 'How does nature work?' 'Why am I me?' If circumstances and temperament allow, we then build on these questions during adulthood, our curiosity encompassing more and more of the world until at some point we may reach that elusive stage where we are bored by nothing. The blunt large questions become connected to smaller, apparently esoteric ones. We end up wondering about flies on the sides of mountains or about a particular fresco on the wall of a sixteenth-century palace. We start to care about the foreign policy of a long-dead Iberian monarch or about the role of peat in the Thirty Years' War.

The chain of questions that led Humboldt to his curiosity about a fly on the ten-inch-wide ledge of Mount Chimborazo in June of 1802 had begun as far back as his eighth year, when, as a boy living in Berlin, he had visited relatives in another part of Germany and asked himself, 'Why don't the same things grow everywhere?' Why were there trees near Berlin that did not grow in Bavaria, and vice versa? His curiosity was encouraged by others. He was given a microscope and a library of books about nature; tutors who understood botany were hired for him. He became known as 'the little chemist' in the family, and his mother hung his drawings of plants on her study wall. By the time he set out for South America, Humboldt was attempting to formulate laws about how flora and fauna were shaped by climate and geography. His seven-year-old's sense of inquiry was still alive within him, but now it was articulated through more sophisticated questions, such as, 'Are ferns affected by northern exposure?' and 'Up to what height will a palm tree survive?'

On descending to the base camp below Mount Chimborazo, Humboldt washed his feet, had a short siesta and almost immediately began writing his 'Essai sur la geographie des plantes', in which he defined the distribution of vegetation at different heights and temperatures. He stated that there were six altitude zones. From sea level to approximately 3,000 feet, palms and pisang plants grew. Up to 4,900 feet there were ferns, and up to 9,200 feet, oak trees. Then came a zone that nurtured evergreen shrubs (*Wintera, Escalloniceae*), followed, on the highest levels, by two alpine zones: between 10,150 and 12,600 feet, herbs grew, and between 12,600 and 14,200 feet, alpine grasses and lichens thrived. Flies were, he wrote excitedly, unlikely to be found above 16,600 feet.

9.

Humboldt's excitement testifies to the importance of having the right question to ask of the world. It may mean the difference between swatting at a fly in irritation and running down a mountain to begin work on an 'Essai sur la geographie des plantes'.

Unfortunately for the traveller, most objects don't come affixed with the question that will generate the excitement they deserve. There is usually nothing fixed to them at all; when there is something, it tends to be the wrong thing. There was a lot fixed to the

	HAUTEURS MESURÉES ou différentes parties DU GLOBE		CULTURE DU SOL		ASPECT		PRESSION de l'Air	TOISES

Géographie des Plantes Equinoxiales from Alexander von Humboldt and Aimé Bonpland's
Tableau physique des Andes et Pays voisins, 1799–1803

Iglesia de San Francisco el Grande, which stood at the end of the long traffic-choked Carrera de San Francisco, but it hardly helped me to be curious about it:

The walls and ceilings of the church are decorated with nineteenth-century frescoes and paintings, except those in the chapels of saints Anthony and Bernardino, which date from the eighteenth century. The Capilla de San Bernardino, the first chapel on the north side, contains in the centre of the wall a Saint Bernardino of Siena preaching before the King of Aragon (1781), painted by Goya as a young man. The sixteenth-century stalls in the sacristy and chapter house come from the Cartuja de El Paular, the Carthusian monastery near Segovia.

The information gave no hint as to how curiosity might arise. It was as mute as the fly on Humboldt's mountain. If a traveller was to feel personally involved with (rather than guiltily obedient towards) 'the walls and ceilings of the church decorated with nineteenth-century frescoes and paintings ...', he or she would have to be able to connect these facts—as boring as a fly—with one of the large, blunt questions to which genuine curiosity must be anchored.

For Humboldt, the question had been, 'Why are there regional variations in nature?' For the person standing before the Iglesia de San Francisco el Grande, the question might be, 'Why have people felt the need to build churches?' or even 'Why do we worship God?' From such a naive starting point, a chain of curiosity would have the chance to grow, involving questions such as 'Why are churches different in different places?', 'What have been the main styles of churches?' and 'Who were the main architects, and why did they achieve success?' Only through such a slow evolution of curiosity

Iglesia de San Francisco el Grande

could a traveller stand a chance of greeting the news that the church's vast neoclassical façade was by Sabatini with anything other than boredom or despair.

A danger of travel is that we may see things at the wrong time, before we have had an opportunity to build up the necessary receptivity, so that new information is as useless and fugitive as necklace beads without a connecting chain.

The risk is compounded by geography, in the way that cities contain buildings or monuments that may be only a few feet apart in space but are leagues apart in terms of what is required to appreciate them. Having made a journey to a place we may never revisit, we feel obliged to admire a sequence of things which have no connection to one another besides a geographic one and a proper understanding of which would require a range of qualities unlikely to be found in any one person. We are asked to be curious about Gothic architecture on one street and then promptly fascinated by Etruscan archaeology on the next.

The visitor to Madrid, for example, is expected to be interested both in the Palacio Real, an eighteenth-century royal residence famed for its chambers decorated with lavish rococo chinoiserie by the Neapolitan designer Gasparini, and—a few moments later—in the Centro de Arte Reina Sofía, a whitewashed gallery devoted to twentieth-century art, whose highlight is Picasso's *Guernica*. Yet the natural progression for someone deepening his or her appreciation of eighteenth-century royal architecture would be to ignore the gallery altogether and head for the palaces of Prague and St Petersburg instead.

Travel twists our curiosity according to a superficial geographical logic, as superficial as if a university course were to prescribe books according to their size rather than subject matter.

10.

Towards the end of his life, his South American adventures long behind him, Humboldt complained, with a mixture of self-pity and pride, 'People often say that I'm curious about too many things at once: botany, astronomy, comparative anatomy. But can you really forbid a man from harbouring a desire to know and embrace everything that surrounds him?'

We cannot, of course, forbid such a thing; a pat on the back feels more appropriate. But our admiration for Humboldt's journey may not preclude our feeling a degree of sympathy for those who, even in the most fascinating cities, have occasionally been visited by a strong wish to remain in bed and take the next flight home.

LANDSCAPE

V

On the Country and the City

Place	*The Lake District*
Guide	*William Wordsworth*

1.

We left London by an afternoon train. I had arranged to meet M. below the departure board at Euston Station. Watching crowds step off the escalators and onto the concourse, I thought it miraculous that in the midst of so many people, I should ever be able to find her—as well as testimony to the strange particularities of desire that it should be precisely she whom I needed to find.

We travelled up the spine of England, and as night fell, there were intimations of countryside, though gradually all we could see was our own faces in windows that had turned into long black mirrors. Somewhere above Stoke-on-Trent I visited the buffet car, sensing once again, on my way through a succession of carriages that swayed as if I were drunk, the excitement caused by the prospect of eating something cooked in a moving train. The timer on the microwave gave off a chunky mechanical sound, like a detonator in an old war film, then rang a dainty bell to signal that it had finished with my hot dog—just as the train went over a level crossing, behind which I could make out the shadow of a group of cows.

We arrived at Oxenholme Station, subtitled 'The Lake District', shortly before nine. Only a few others alighted with us, and we walked silently along the platform, our breaths visible in the night chill. Back inside the train, passengers were dozing or reading. The Lake District would, for them, be one stop among many, a place where they would look up from their books for a moment and take in the concrete pots arranged symmetrically along the platform, check the station clock and perhaps let out uninhibited yawns before the Glasgow train pulled off again into the darkness and they returned to a new paragraph.

The station was deserted, though it could not always have been thus, for unusually many of the signs were subtitled in Japanese. We had called from London to rent a car and found it at the end of a parking bay, under a street lamp. The rental company had run out of the small models we had asked for, and had delivered instead a large burgundy family saloon that had a heady new-car smell to it, and an immaculate grey carpet across which the marks of a vacuum cleaner were still visible.

2.

The immediate motives for our journey were personal, but they might also be said to have belonged to a broader historical movement dating back to the second half of the eighteenth century, in which city dwellers began for the first time to travel in great numbers through the countryside in an attempt to restore health to their bodies and, more important, harmony to their souls. In the year 1700, 17 percent of the population of England and Wales lived in cities and towns. By 1850, 50 percent did, and by 1900, 75 percent.

We headed north towards the village of Troutbeck, a few miles above Lake Windermere. We had reserved a room at an inn called the Mortal Man, where two narrow beds with stained blankets had been pushed together. The landlord showed us the bathroom, warned us of the high phone charges, which he suspected (from our clothes and our hesitant manner at the reception desk) we would be unable to afford, and, as he took his leave, promised us three days of perfect weather and welcomed us to the Lake District.

We tried the television and found news from London but after a moment switched it off and opened the window instead. There was an owl hooting outside, and we thought of its strange existence, out there in the otherwise silent night.

I had come in part because of a poet. That evening in our room, I read another section of Wordsworth's *Prelude*. The cover of the paperback was illustrated with a portrait by Benjamin Haydon, which showed Wordsworth severe and aged. M. declared him an old toad and went to have a bath, though later, while standing by the window applying face cream, she recited several lines from a poem whose title she had forgotten, which she said had moved her perhaps more than anything else she had ever read:

> *What though the radiance which was once so bright*
> *Be now for ever taken from my sight,*
>   *Though nothing can bring back the hour*
> *Of splendour in the grass, of glory in the flower;*
>   *We will grieve not, rather find*
>   *Strength in what remains behind*

Ode, Intimations of Immortality

We went to bed, and I tried to read further, though it became hard to concentrate after I found a long blond hair caught on the headboard that belonged neither to M. nor to me and hinted at the many guests who had stayed in the Mortal Man before us, one of whom was perhaps now on another continent, unaware of having left a part of herself behind. We fell into fitful sleep to the sound of the owl outside.

3.

William Wordsworth was born in 1770 in the small town of Cockermouth on the northern edge of the Lake District. He spent, in his words, 'half his boyhood in running wild among the Mountains' and aside from interludes in London and Cambridge and travels around Europe, lived his whole life in the Lake District, first in a modest

two-storeyed stone dwelling, Dove Cottage in the village of Grasmere, and then, as his fame increased, in a more substantial home in
nearby Rydal.

And almost every day, he went on a long walk in the mountains or
along the lakeshore. He was unbothered by the rain that, as he
admitted, tended to fall in the Lake District 'with a vigour and perseverance that may remind the disappointed traveller of those del-
uges of rain which fall among the Abyssinian mountains for the
annual supply of the Nile'. His acquaintance Thomas De Quincey
would estimate that Wordsworth had walked between 175,000 and
180,000 miles over his lifetime—a statistic that was all the more
remarkable, added De Quincey, considering his physique: 'For
Wordsworth was, upon the whole, not a well-made man. His legs
were pointedly condemned by all the female connoisseurs in legs
that I ever heard lecture upon the topic.' Sadly, De Quincey continued, 'the total effect of Wordsworth's person was always worst in a
state of motion, for, according to the remark I have heard from many
country people, "he walked like a cade"—a cade being some sort of
insect which advances by an oblique motion.'

It was during his cadelike walks that Wordsworth derived the
inspiration for many of his works, including 'To a Butterfly', 'To
the Cuckoo', 'To a Skylark', 'To the Daisy' and 'To the Small
Celandine'—poems about natural phenomena that poets had hitherto looked at only casually or ritualistically, if at all, but that
Wordsworth now declared to be the noblest subjects of his craft. On
the sixteenth of March 1802—according to the journal of his sister,
Dorothy, who kept a record of her sibling's movements around the
Lake District—Wordsworth walked across a bridge at Brothers
Water, a placid lake near Patterdale, and then sat down to write the
following:

The cock is crowing
The stream is flowing
The small birds twitter,
The lake doth glitter . . .
There's joy in the mountains;
There's life in the fountains;
Small clouds are sailing,
Blue sky prevailing

A few weeks afterwards, the poet found himself moved to write by the beauty of a sparrow's nest:

Look, five blue eggs are gleaming there!
Few visions have I seen more fair,
Nor many prospects of delight
More pleasing than that simple sight!

He experienced the same need to express joy a few summers later on hearing the sound of a nightingale:

O Nightingale! thou surely art
A Creature of a fiery heart—. . .
Thou sing'st as if the God of wine
Had help'd thee to a Valentine.

These were not haphazard articulations of pleasure. Behind them lay a well-developed philosophy of nature, which—infusing all of Wordsworth's work—made an original and, in the history of Western thought, hugely influential claim about our requirements for happiness and the origins of our unhappiness. The poet proposed that nature—which he took to comprise, among other elements, birds, streams, daffodils and sheep—was an indispensable corrective to the psychological damage inflicted by life in the city.

The message met with vicious initial resistance. Lord Byron, reviewing Wordsworth's *Poems in Two Volumes* in 1807, was bewildered that a grown man could make such claims on behalf of flowers and animals: 'What will any reader out of the nursery say to such namby-pamby … an imitation of such minstrelsy as soothed our cries in the cradle?' The editors of the *Edinburgh Review* concurred, declaring Wordsworth's poetry 'a piece of babyish absurdity' and wondering whether it might not represent a deliberate attempt by the author to turn himself into a laughingstock: 'It is possible that the sight of a garden spade or a sparrow's nest might really have suggested to Wordsworth a train of powerful impressions … but it is certain that to most minds, such associations will always appear forced, strained and unnatural. All the world laughs at 'Elegiac Stanzas to a Suckling-Pig', 'A Hymn on Washing-Day', 'Sonnets to One's Grandmother', or 'Pindaric Odes on Gooseberry-Pie'; and yet, it seems, it is not easy to convince Mr Wordsworth of this.'

Parodies of the poet's work soon began to circulate in the literary journals.

When I see a cloud,
I think out loud,
How lovely it is,
To see the sky like this

ran one.

Was it a robin that I saw?
Was it a pigeon or a daw?

ran another.

Wordsworth was stoic. 'Trouble not yourself upon the present reception of these poems,' he advised Lady Beaumont. 'Of what moment is that when compared with what I trust is their destiny, to console the afflicted, to add sunshine to daylight by making the happy happier, to teach the young and the gracious of every age to see, to think and feel, and therefore to become more actively and securely virtuous; this is their office, which I trust they will faithfully perform long after we (that is, all that is mortal of us) are mouldered in our graves.'

He was wrong only about how long it would take. 'Up to 1820, the name of Wordsworth was trampled under foot,' explained De Quincey. 'From 1820 to 1830 it was militant; and from 1830 to 1835 it has been triumphant.' Taste underwent a slow but radical transformation. The reading public gradually ceased guffawing and learnt to be charmed and even to recite by heart hymns to butterflies and sonnets on celandines. Wordsworth's poetry attracted tourists to the places that had inspired it. New hotels were opened in Windermere, Rydal and Grasmere. By 1845, it was estimated that there were more tourists in the Lake District than there were sheep. They prized glimpses of the cadeish creature in his garden in Rydal, and on hillsides and lakeshores sought out the sites whose power he had described in verse. On the death of Southey, in 1843, Wordsworth was appointed England's poet laureate. Plans were drawn up by a group of well-wishers in London to have the Lake District renamed Wordsworthshire.

By the time of the poet's death at the age of eighty, in 1850 (by which year half of the population of England and Wales was urban), serious critical opinion seemed almost universally sympathetic to his suggestion that regular travel through nature was a necessary antidote to the evils of the city.

4.

Part of Wordsworth's complaint was directed towards the smoke, congestion, poverty and ugliness of cities, but clean-air bills and slum clearance would not by themselves have eradicated his critique. For it was the effect of cities on our souls, rather than on our health, that concerned him.

The poet accused cities of fostering a family of life-destroying emotions: anxiety about our position in the social hierarchy, envy at the success of others, pride and a desire to shine in the eyes of strangers. City dwellers had no perspective, he alleged, they were in thrall to what was spoken of in the street or at the dinner table. However well provided for, they had a relentless desire for new things, which they did not genuinely lack and on which their happiness did not depend. And in this crowded, anxious sphere, it seemed harder than it did on an isolated homestead to begin sincere relationships with others. 'One thought baffled my understanding,' wrote Wordsworth of his residence in London: 'How men lived even next-door neighbours, as we say, yet still strangers, and knowing not each other's names.'

Myself afflicted by a few of these ills, I had, one evening several months before my journey to the Lake District, emerged from a gathering held in the centre of London, that 'turbulent world/of men and things' (*The Prelude*). Walking away from the venue, envious and worried about my position, I found myself deriving unexpected

relief from the sight of a vast object overhead, which, in spite of the darkness, I attempted to photograph with a pocket camera—and which served to bring home to me, as rarely before, the redemptive power of natural forces with which so much of Wordsworth's poetry is concerned.

The cloud had floated over that part of the city only a few minutes before and, given the strong westerly wind, was not destined to remain above it long. The lights of surrounding offices lent to its edges an almost decadent fluorescent orange glow, making it look like a grave old man bedecked with party decorations, and yet its granite-grey centre testified to its origins in the slow interplay of air and sea. Soon it would be over the fields of Essex, then the marshes and oil refineries, before heading out over the mutinous North Sea waves.

Keeping my eyes fixed on the apparition while walking towards the bus stop, I felt my anxieties abate, and I turned over in my mind some lines the cadeish poet once composed in honour of a Welsh valley:

> *... [Nature] can so inform*
> *The mind that is within us, so impress*
> *With quietness and beauty, and so feed*
> *With lofty thoughts, that neither evil tongues,*
> *Rash judgments, nor the sneers of selfish men,*
> *Nor greetings where no kindness is, nor all*
> *The dreary intercourse of daily life,*
> *Shall e'er prevail against us, or disturb*
> *Our chearful faith that all which we behold*
> *Is full of blessings.*

Lines Written a Few Miles above Tintern Abbey

5.

In the summer of 1798, Wordsworth and his sister went on a walking holiday along the Wye Valley in Wales, where William had a moment of revelation about the power of nature that was to resonate through his poetry for the rest of his life. It was his second visit to the valley; he had walked along it five years before. In the intervening period he had endured a succession of unhappy experiences: he had spent time in London, a city he feared; altered his political views by reading Godwin; transformed his sense of a poet's mission through his friendship with Coleridge and travelled across a revolutionary France wrecked by Robespierre's Great Terror.

Back in Wye, Wordsworth found an elevated spot where he sat down under a sycamore tree, looked out across the valley and its river, cliffs, hedgerows and forests and was inspired to write perhaps his greatest poem. At least, 'no poem of mine was composed under circumstances more pleasant for me to remember than this', he would later explain of 'Lines Written a Few Miles above Tintern Abbey', which he subtitled 'On revisiting the banks of the Wye during a Tour, July 13, 1798', an ode to the restorative powers of nature.

> *Though absent long,*
> *These forms of beauty have not been to me,*
> *As is a landscape to a blind man's eye:*
> *But oft, in lonely rooms, and mid the din*
> *Of towns and cities, I have owed to them,*
> *In hours of weariness, sensations sweet . . .*
> *With tranquil restoration.*

Philip James de Loutherbourg, *The River Wye at Tintern Abbey*, 1805

The dichotomy of town and country forms the backbone of the poem, with the latter repeatedly being invoked as a counter to the pernicious influence of the former:

> how oft,
> In darkness, and amid the many shapes
> Of joyless day-light; when the fretful stir
> Unprofitable, and the fever of the world,—
> Have hung upon the beatings of my heart,
> How oft, in spirit, have I turned to thee
> O sylvan Wye! Thou wanderer through the woods,
> How often has my spirit turned to thee!

This expression of gratitude was to recur in *The Prelude*, where the poet once more acknowledged his debt to nature for enabling him to dwell in the cities without succumbing to the base emotions that, he held, they habitually fostered:

> If, mingling with the world, I am content
> With my own modest pleasures, and have lived ...
> removed
> From little enmities and low desires,
> The gift is yours ...
> Ye winds and sounding cataracts! 'tis yours,
> Ye mountains! thine, O Nature!

6.
Why? Why would proximity to a cataract, a mountain or any other form of nature render one any less likely to experience 'enmities and low desires' than proximity to crowded streets?

The Lake District offered suggestions. M. and I rose early on our first morning and went down to the Mortal Man's breakfast room, which was painted pink and overlooked a luxuriant valley. It was raining heavily, but the landlord assured us, before serving us porridge and informing us that eggs would cost extra, that this was but a passing shower. A tape recorder was playing Peruvian pipe music, interspersed with highlights of Handel's *Messiah*. Having eaten, we packed a rucksack and drove to the town of Ambleside, where we bought a few items to take with us on a walk: a compass, a waterproof map holder, water, chocolate and some sandwiches.

Little Ambleside had the bustle of a metropolis. Lorries were noisily unloading their goods outside shops, there were placards everywhere advertising restaurants and hotels, and though it was still early, the tea shops were full. On racks outside newsagents' stalls, the papers reported on the latest development in a political scandal in London.

A few miles northwest of the town, in the Great Langdale Valley, the atmosphere was transformed. For the first time since arriving in the Lake District, we were in deep countryside, where nature was more in evidence than humans. On either side of the path stood a number of oak trees. Each one grew far from the shadow of its neighbour, in fields so appetising to sheep as to have been eaten down to a perfect lawn. The oaks were of noble bearing: they did not trail their branches on the ground as willows are wont to do, nor did their leaves have the dishevelled appearance common to certain poplars, which can look from close up as though they have been awoken in the middle of the night and not had time to fix their hair. Instead they gathered their lower branches tightly under themselves, while their upper branches grew in small, orderly steps. The result was a rich green foliage in an almost perfect circle, like an archetypal tree drawn by a child.

The rain, which continued to fall confidently despite the promises of the landlord, gave us a sense of the mass of the oaks. From under their damp canopy, rain could be heard falling on forty thousand leaves, creating a harmonious pitter-patter that varied in pitch according to whether the water dripped onto a large or a small leaf, a high or a low one, one loaded with accumulated water or not. The trees themselves were an image of ordered complexity: the roots patiently drew nutrients from the soil, and the capillaries of the trunks sent water twenty-five metres upwards, each branch taking enough but not too much for the needs of its own leaves, each leaf in turn contributing to the maintenance of the whole. The trees were an image of patience, for they would sit out this rainy morning and the many that would follow it without complaint, adjusting themselves to the slow shift of the seasons, showing no ill temper in a storm, no desire to wander from their spot for an impetuous journey across to another valley—content to keep their many slender fingers deep in the clammy soil, metres from their central stems and far from those tallest leaves that held the rainwater in their palms.

Wordsworth enjoyed sitting beneath oaks, listening to the rain or watching sunbeams fracture across their leaves. What he saw as the patience and dignity of the trees seemed to him characteristic of nature's works, which were to be valued for holding up,

> *before the mind intoxicate*
> *With present objects, and the busy dance*
> *Of things that pass away, a temperate show*
> *Of objects that endure.*

Nature would, he proposed, dispose us to seek out in life and in one another 'whate'er there is desirable and good'. An 'image of right reason', nature would temper the crooked impulses of urban life.

If we are to accept (even in part) Wordsworth's argument, we may need to concede a prior principle holding that our identities are to a greater or lesser extent malleable, changing according to whom—and sometimes *what*—we are with. The company of certain people may excite our generosity and sensitivity, while that of others awakens our competitiveness and envy. Thus A's obsession with status and hierarchy may—almost imperceptibly—lead B to worry about his own significance, even as A's jokes quietly rouse his hitherto submerged sense of the ridiculous. But move B to another environment, and his concerns will subtly shift in response to a new interlocutor.

What, then, may be expected to happen to a person's identity in the company of a cataract or a mountain, an oak tree or a celandine, objects that after all have no conscious concerns and so, it would seem, can neither encourage nor censor particular behaviours? And yet an inanimate object may, to come to the linchpin of Wordsworth's claim for the beneficial effects of nature, still work an influence on those around it. Natural scenes have the power to suggest certain values to us—oaks dignity, pines resolution, lakes calm—and therefore may, in unobtrusive ways, act as inspirations to virtue.

In a letter written to a young student in the summer of 1802, addressing the task of poetry, Wordsworth came close to specifying the values that he felt nature embodied: 'A great Poet ... ought to a certain degree to rectify men's feelings ... to render their feelings more *sane, pure and permanent*, in short, more consonant to Nature.'

In every natural landscape, Wordsworth found instances of such sanity, purity and permanence. Flowers, for example, were models of humility and meekness:

Sweet silent Creature!
That breath'st with me in sun and air,
Do thou, as thou art wont, repair
My heart with gladness, and a share
  Of thy meek nature!

Animals, for their part, were paragons of stoicism. Wordsworth at one point became quite attached to a bluetit that even in the worst weather sang in the orchard above Dove Cottage. During their first, freezing winter there, the poet and his sister were inspired by a pair of swans that were also new to the area, and that endured the cold with greater patience than the Wordsworths.

An hour up the Langdale Valley, the rain having abated, M. and I hear a faint *tseep,* rapidly repeated, alternating with a louder *tissip.* Three meadow pipits are flying out of a patch of rough grass. A black-eared wheatear is looking pensive on a conifer branch, warming its pale sandy-buff feathers in the late-summer sun. Stirred by something, it takes off and circles the valley, releasing a rapid and high-pitched *schwer, schwee, schwee-oo.* The sound has no effect on a caterpillar that was walking strenuously across a rock, nor on the many sheep dotted across the valley floor.

One of the sheep ambles towards the path and looks curiously at his visitors. Humans and sheep stare at each other in wonder. After a moment, the sheep sinks into a reclining pose and takes a lazy mouthful of grass, which he chews on one side of his mouth, as if it were gum. What makes me me and him him? Another sheep approaches and lies down next to his companion, wool to wool, and for a second they exchange what appears to be a knowing, mildly amused glance.

A few meters ahead, from inside a deep-green bush that runs down to a stream comes a noise like the sound of a lethargic old man clearing his throat after a heavy lunch. It is followed by an incongruously frantic rustle, as though someone was rifling through a bed of leaves in an irritated search for a valuable possession. But on noticing that it has company, the creature falls silent—the tense silence of a child holding his or her breath at the back of a clothes cupboard during a game of hide-and-seek. Back in Ambleside, people are buying newspapers and eating scones, while out here, buried in a bush, is a thing, probably with fur and perhaps a tail, interested in eating berries or flies, scurrying in the foliage and grunting—and yet still, for all its oddities, a *contemporary*, a fellow sleeping and breathing creature alive on this singular planet in a universe otherwise made up chiefly of rocks and vapours and silence.

One of Wordsworth's poetic ambitions was to induce us to see the many animals living alongside us that we typically ignore, registering them only out of the corner of our eyes and feeling no appreciation for what they are up to and want: shadowy, generic presences such as the bird up on the steeple and the rustling creature in the bush. He invited his readers to abandon their usual perspectives and to consider for a time how the world might look through other eyes, to shuttle between the human and the natural perspective. Why might this be interesting, or even inspiring? Perhaps because unhappiness can stem from having only one perspective to play with. A few days before travelling to the Lake District, I had happened upon a nineteenth-century book that discussed Wordsworth's interest in birds and in its preface hinted at the benefits of the alternative perspective they offered: 'I am sure it would give much pleasure to many of the public if the local, daily and weekly press throughout this country would always record, not only the arrivals and departures of Lords, Ladies, M.P's and the great people of this land, but also the arrivals and departures of birds.' If we are pained by the values of the age or of the elite, it may be a source of relief for us to come upon reminders of the diversity of life on our planet, to hold in mind that alongside the business of the great people of the land, there are also pipits *tseep*ing in meadows.

Looking back on Wordsworth's early poems, Coleridge would assert that their genius had been to 'give the charm of novelty to things of every day, and to excite a feeling analogous to the supernatural, by awakening the mind's attention from the lethargy of custom, and directing it to the loveliness and wonders of the world before us; an inexhaustible treasure, but for which, in consequence of the film of familiarity and selfish solicitude[,] we have eyes, yet see not, ears that hear not, and hearts that neither feel nor understand.' Nature's 'loveliness' might in turn, according to Wordsworth, encourage us to locate the good in ourselves. Two people standing on the edge of a rock overlooking a stream and a grand wooded valley might thus transform their relationship not just with nature but also, and just as significantly, with each other.

There are concerns that seem indecent when one is in the company of a cliff, and others to which cliffs naturally lend their assistance, their majesty encouraging the steady and high-minded in ourselves, their size teaching us to respect with good grace and an awed humility all that surpasses us. It is of course still possible to feel envy for a colleague before a mighty cataract, but if the Wordsworthian message is to be believed, it is a little more unlikely. Wordsworth argued that through a life spent in nature, his character

Asher Brown Durand, *Kindred Spirits*, 1849

had been shaped to resist competition, envy and anxiety—and so he celebrated

>   *... that first I looked*
> *At Man through objects that were great or fair;*
> *First communed with him by their help. And thus*
> *Was founded a sure safeguard and defence*
> *Against the weight of meanness, selfish cares,*
> *Coarse manners, vulgar passions, that beat in*
> *On all sides from the ordinary world*
> *In which we traffic.*

7.

M. and I were unable to stay long in the Lake District. Three days after our arrival, we were back on the London train, seated opposite a man who was making calls on his mobile phone in a vain search, as the carriage learnt during conversations extending across many fields and industrial cities, for someone called Jim, who owed him money.

Even if we allow how beneficial contact with nature may be, we recognize that its effects must surely be of limited duration. Three days in nature can scarcely be expected to work a psychological effect lasting longer than a few hours.

Wordsworth, however, was less pessimistic. In the autumn of 1790, the poet went on a walking tour of the Alps. He travelled from Geneva to the Vale of Chamouni, then crossed the Simplon Pass and descended through the Ravine of Gondo to Lake Maggiore. In a letter to his sister describing what he had seen, he wrote, 'At this moment when many of these landscapes are floating before my mind, I feel a high enjoyment in reflecting that perhaps *scarce a day of my life* will pass in which I shall not derive some happiness from these images' (emphasis added).

This was no hyperbole. Decades later, the Alps would continue to live within him and to strengthen his spirit whenever he evoked them. Their survival led him to argue that we may see in nature certain scenes that will stay with us throughout our lives and offer us, every time they enter our consciousness, both a contrast to and relief from present difficulties. He termed such experiences in nature 'spots of time':

> *There are in our existence spots of time,*
> *That with distinct pre-eminence retain*
> *A renovating virtue . . .*
> *That penetrates, enables us to mount,*
> *When high, more high, and lifts us up when fallen.*

This belief in small, critical moments in nature explains Wordsworth's unusually specific way of subtitling many of his poems. The subtitle of 'Tintern Abbey', for example—'On revisiting the banks of the Wye during a tour, July 13, 1798'—cites an exact day, month and year to suggest that a few moments in the countryside overlooking a valley could number among the most significant and useful of one's life, and be as worthy of precise remembrance as a birthday or a wedding.

I, too, was granted a 'spot of time'. It occurred in the late afternoon of the second day of our visit to the Lake District. M. and I were sitting on a bench near Ambleside eating chocolate bars. We had exchanged a few words about which kinds of chocolate bars we preferred. M. said she liked caramel-filled ones, I expressed a greater interest in the dry, biscuity sort, and then we fell silent and I looked out across a field to a clump of trees by a stream. There were a host of different colours in the trees, sharp gradations of green, as if someone had fanned out samples from a colour chart. These trees gave off an impression of astonishing health and exuberance. They seemed not to care that the world was old and often sad. I was tempted to bury my face in them so as to be restored by their smell. It seemed extraordinary that nature could on its own, without any concern for the happiness of two people eating chocolate on a bench, have come up with a scene so utterly suited to a human sense of beauty and proportion.

My receptivity to the scene lasted only a minute. Thoughts of work then intruded, and M. suggested that we return to the inn so she could make a phone call. I was unaware of having fixed the scene in my memory until, one midafternoon in London, I was waiting in a traffic jam, oppressed by cares, and the trees came back to me, pushing aside a raft of meetings and unanswered correspondence and asserting themselves in my consciousness. I was carried away from the traffic and the crowds and returned to trees whose names I didn't know but which I could see as clearly as if they were standing before me. These trees provided a ledge against which I could rest my thoughts; they protected me from the eddies of anxiety and, in a small way that afternoon, contributed a reason to be alive.

At eleven o'clock in the morning on 15 April 1802, Wordsworth saw some daffodils along the western shore of Ullswater Lake, a few miles north of where M. and I stayed. There were some ten thousand of these flowers 'dancing in the breeze', he wrote. The waves of the lake seemed to dance beside them, too, though the daffodils 'outdid the sparkling waves in glee'. 'What wealth the shew to me had brought', he explained of a moment that would become, for him, a spot of time:

For oft when on my couch I lie
In vacant or in pensive mood.
They flash upon that inward eye…
And then my heart with pleasure fills,
And dances with the Daffodils.

An unfortunate last line perhaps, open to Byronic accusations of being 'namby-pamby', but nevertheless offering the consoling idea that in vacant or pensive moods, in traffic in the city's 'turbulent world', we may also draw on images of our travels through nature, images of a group of trees or a spread of daffodils on the shores of a lake, and with their help, blunt a little the forces of 'enmity and low desires'.

On Travelling in the Lake District,
14–18 September 2000

VI

On the Sublime

Place	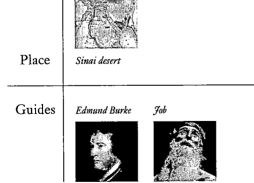 *Sinai desert*
Guides	*Edmund Burke* *Job*

1.

Long partial to deserts, drawn to photographs of the American West (bits of tumbleweed blowing across a wasteland) and the names of the great deserts (Mojave, Kalahari, Taklamakan, Gobi), I booked a charter flight to the Israeli resort of Eilat and went to wander in the Sinai. On the plane journey over, I talked to a young Australian woman beside me, who was taking up a job as a lifeguard at the Eilat Hilton, and I read Pascal:

When I consider ... the small space I occupy, which I see swallowed up in the infinite immensity of spaces of which I know nothing and which know nothing of me [l'infinie immensité des espaces que j'ignore et qui m'ignorent], *I take fright and am amazed to see myself here rather than there: there is no reason for me to be here rather than there, now rather than then. Who put me here?*

Pascal, *Pensées*, 68

Wordsworth urged us to travel through landscapes in order to feel emotions that may benefit our souls. I set out for the desert so as to be made to feel small.

It is usually unpleasant to be made to feel small, whether by doormen in hotels or by comparison with heroes of great achievement. But there may be another and more satisfying way for a person to feel diminished. Intimations of this may be felt by any viewer who stands in front of *Rocky Mountains, Landers Peak* (1863) by Albert Bierstadt, *An Avalanche in the Alps* (1803) by Philip James de Loutherbourg or *Chalk Cliffs on Rügen* by Caspar David Friedrich. What do such barren, overwhelming spaces do for us?

Albert Bierstadt, *Rocky Mountains, Landers Peak*, 1863

2.

Two days into my Sinai trip, the group of twelve that I have joined reaches a valley empty of life, without trees, grass, water or animals. Only boulders lie strewn across its sandstone floor, as though the stamping of a petulant giant had caused them to roll off the sides of the surrounding mountains. These mountains look like naked Alps, their nudity revealing geological origins normally concealed beneath coats of earth and pine forest. There are gashes and fissures that speak of the pressures of millennia, offering up cross sections through disproportionate expanses of time. The Earth's tectonic plates have rippled granite as though it were linen. The mountains spread out in seeming infinity over the horizon until eventually the high plateau of the southern Sinai gives way to a featureless, baking gravel pan to which the Bedouins have given the name El Tih, or the 'Desert of the Wandering'.

3.

There are few emotions about places for which adequate single words exist; we are forced instead to make awkward piles of words to convey what we feel as we watch the light fade on an early-autumn evening, or when we encounter a pool of perfectly still water in a clearing.

But at the beginning of the eighteenth century, a word came to prominence by means of which it became possible to indicate a specific response towards precipices and glaciers, night skies and boulder-strewn deserts. In their presence one was likely to experience, and could count on being understood if one reported that one had felt, a sense of the sublime.

Philip James de Loutherbourg, *An Avalanche in the Alps*, 1803

Caspar David Friedrich, *Chalk Cliffs on Rügen, c.* 1818

The word itself had originated around 200 A.D., in a treatise 'On the Sublime' ascribed to the Greek author Longinus, but it had languished until a retranslation of the essay into English in 1712 sparked renewed, intense interest among critics. While these writers often differed in their specific analyses of the word, their shared assumptions were striking. They grouped into a single category, by virtue of their size, emptiness or danger, a variety of hitherto unconnected landscapes, and argued that such places provoked an identifiable feeling that was both pleasurable and morally good. The value of landscapes would henceforth be decided not solely on the basis of formal aesthetic criteria (the harmony of colours, for example, or the arrangement of lines) or even economic or practical concerns, but rather according to the power of places to arouse the mind to sublimity.

Joseph Addison, in his 'Essay on the Pleasures of the Imagination', wrote of the 'delightful stillness and amazement' he felt before 'the prospects of an open champian country, a vast uncultivated desert, huge heaps of mountains, high rocks and precipices and a wide expanse of waters'. Hildebrand Jacob, in an essay entitled 'How the Mind Is Raised by the Sublime', offered a list of the places and things that were most likely to invoke this prized feeling: oceans, either in calm or storm, the setting sun, precipices, caverns and Swiss mountains.

Travellers set off to investigate. In 1739, the poet Thomas Gray undertook a walking tour of the Alps, the first of many such self-conscious pursuits of the sublime, and afterwards reported, 'In our little journey up to the Grande Chartreuse, I do not remember to have gone ten paces without an exclamation that there was no restraining. Not a precipice, not a torrent, not a cliff, but is pregnant with religion and poetry.'

4.

The southern Sinai at dawn. What, then, is this feeling? It is generated by a valley created four hundred million years ago, by a granite mountain 2,300 meters high and by the erosion of millennia marked on the walls of a succession of steep canyons. Beside all these, man seems merely dust postponed: the sublime as an encounter—pleasurable; intoxicating, even—with human weakness in the face of the strength, age and size of the universe.

In my backpack, I am carrying a torch, a sun hat and Edmund Burke. At the age of twenty-four, after giving up his legal studies in London, Burke composed *A Philosophical Enquiry into the Origin of Our Ideas of the Sublime and Beautiful.* He was categorical: sublimity had to do with a feeling of weakness. Many landscapes were beautiful—meadows in spring, soft valleys, oak trees, banks of flowers (daisies especially)—but they were not sublime. 'The ideas of the sublime and beautiful are frequently confounded,' he complained. 'Both are indiscriminately applied to things greatly differing and sometimes of natures directly opposite'—a trace of irritation on the part of the young philosopher with those who might have gasped at the Thames from Kew and called that sublime. A landscape could arouse the sublime only when it suggested power—a power greater than that of humans, and threatening to them. Sublime places embodied a defiance to man's will. Burke illustrated his argument with an analogy about oxen and bulls: 'An ox is a creature of vast strength; but he is an innocent creature, extremely serviceable, and not at all dangerous; for which reason the idea of an ox is by no means grand. A bull is strong too; but his strength is of another kind; often very destructive.... The idea of a bull is therefore great, and it has frequently a place in sublime descriptions, and elevating comparisons.'

There were oxlike landscapes, innocent and 'not all dangerous', pliable to human will; Burke had spent his youth in one such, at a Quaker boarding school in the village of Ballitore in County Kildare, thirty miles southwest of Dublin: a landscape of farms, orchards, hedges, rivers and gardens. Then there were bull-like landscapes. The essayist enumerated their qualities: they were vast, empty, often dark and apparently infinite because of the uniformity and succession of their elements. The Sinai was among them.

5.

But why the pleasure? Why seek out this feeling of smallness—delight in it, even? Why leave the comforts of Eilat, join a group of desert devotees and walk for miles with a heavy pack along the shores of the Gulf of Aqaba, all to reach a place of rocks and silence where one must shelter from the sun like a fugitive in the scant shadow of giant boulders? Why contemplate with exhilaration rather than despair beds of granite and baking gravel pans and a frozen lava of mountains extending into the distance until the peaks dissolve at the edge of a hard blue sky?

One answer is that not everything that is more powerful than us must always be hateful to us. What defies our will can provoke anger and resentment, but it may also arouse awe and respect. It depends on whether the obstacle appears noble in its defiance or squalid and insolent. We begrudge the defiance of the cocky doorman even as we honour that of the mist-shrouded mountain. We are humiliated by what is powerful and mean but awed by what is powerful and noble. To return to and extend Burke's animal analogy, a bull may arouse a feeling of the sublime, whereas a piranha cannot. It seems a matter of motives: we interpret the piranha's power as being vicious and predatory, and the bull's as guileless and impersonal.

Even when we are not in deserts, the behaviour of others and our own flaws are prone to leave us feeling small. Humiliation is a perpetual risk in the world of men. It is not unusual for our will to be defied and our wishes frustrated. Sublime landscapes do not therefore introduce us to our inadequacy; rather, to touch on the crux of their appeal, they allow us to conceive of a familiar inadequacy in a new and more helpful way. Sublime places repeat in grand terms a lesson that ordinary life typically introduces viciously: that the universe is mightier than we are, that we are frail and temporary and have no alternative but to accept limitations on our will; that we must bow to necessities greater than ourselves.

This is the lesson written into the stones of the desert and the ice fields of the poles. So grandly is it written there that we may come away from such places not crushed but inspired by what lies beyond us, privileged to be subject to such majestic necessities. The sense of awe may even shade into a desire to worship.

6.

Because what is mightier than man has traditionally been called God, it does not seem unusual to start thinking of a deity in the Sinai. The mountains and valleys spontaneously suggest that the planet was built by something other than our own hands, by a force greater than we could gather, long before we were born, and set to continue long after our extinction (something we may forget when there are flowers and fast-food restaurants by the roadside).

God is said to have spent much time in the Sinai, most notably two years in the central region, looking after a group of irascible Israelites who complained about the lack of food and had a weakness for foreign gods. 'The Lord came from Sinai,' said Moses shortly before his death (Deuteronomy 33:2). 'And Mount Sinai was altogether on a smoke, because the LORD descended upon it in fire: and the smoke thereof ascended as the smoke of a furnace, and the whole mount quaked greatly,' we are told by Exodus (19:18). 'And all the people saw the thunderings, and the lightnings, and the noise of the trumpet, and the mountain smoking: and when the people saw it, they removed and stood afar off. And Moses said unto the people, Fear not: for God is come to prove you ...' (Exodus 20:18–19).

But biblical history serves only to reinforce an impression that would have occurred anyway to a traveller encamped in the Sinai: an impression that some intentional being must have had a hand in this, something greater than man and with an intelligence that mere 'nature' does not possess—a 'something' for which the word *God* still seems, even to the secular mind, a far from unlikely appellation. The knowledge that natural rather than supernatural forces can also create beauty and an impression of power seems peculiarly ineffective when one stands before a sandstone valley rising towards what appears to be a giant altar, above which hangs a slender crescent moon.

Early writers on the sublime repeatedly connected sublime landscapes with religion:

- Joseph Addison, 'On the Pleasures of the Imagination' (1712): 'A vast space naturally raises in my thoughts the idea of an Almighty Being.'
- Thomas Gray, *Letters* (1739): 'There are certain scenes that would awe an atheist into belief without the help of any other argument.'
- Thomas Cole, 'Essay on American Scenery' (1835): 'Amid those scenes of solitude from which the hand of nature has never been lifted, the associations are of God the creator—they are

his undefiled works, and the mind is cast into the contemplation of eternal things.'

- Ralph Waldo Emerson, 'Nature' (1836): 'The noblest ministry of nature is to stand as the apparition of God.'

.

It is no coincidence that the Western attraction to sublime landscapes developed at precisely the moment when traditional beliefs in God began to wane. It is as if these landscapes allowed travellers to experience transcendent feelings that they no longer felt in cities and the cultivated countryside. The landscapes offered them an emotional connection to a greater power, even as they freed them of the need to subscribe to the more specific and now less plausible claims of biblical texts and organised religions.

7.

The link between God and sublime landscapes is made most explicit in one book of the Bible. The circumstances are peculiar: God is asked by a righteous but desperate man to explain why his life has become full of suffering. And God answers him by bidding him to contemplate the deserts and the mountains, rivers and ice caps, oceans and skies. Seldom have sublime places been asked to bear the burden of such a weighty, urgent question.

At the beginning of the Book of Job, described by Edmund Burke as the most sublime book of the Old Testament, we learn that Job was a wealthy, devout man from the land of Uz. He had seven sons, three daughters, seven thousand sheep, three thousand camels, five hundred yoke of oxen and five hundred donkeys. His wishes were obeyed, and his virtue was rewarded. Then one day disaster struck. The Sabaeans stole Job's oxen and asses, lightning killed his sheep and the Chaldeans raided his camels. A hurricane blew in from the desert and wrecked the house of his eldest son, killing him and his siblings. Painful sores developed from the soles of Job's feet to the top of his head, and, as he sat in the ashes of his house, he scratched them with a piece of broken pottery and wept.

Why had Job been so afflicted? His friends had the answer: he had sinned. Bildad the Shuhite told Job that his children could not have been killed by God unless they and Job himself had done wrong. 'God will not reject a righteous man,' said Bildad. Zophar the Naamathite ventured that God must have been generous in his treatment of Job: 'Know therefore that God exacteth of thee less than thine iniquity deserveth.'

But Job could not accept these words. He called them 'proverbs of ashes' and 'defences of clay'. He had not been a bad man—so why had bad things happened to him?

It is one of the most acute questions asked of God in all the books of the Old Testament. And from a whirlwind in the desert, a furious God answers Job as follows:

Who is this that darkeneth counsel by words without knowledge?

Gird up now thy loins like a man; for I will demand of thee, and answer thou me.

Where was thou when I laid the foundations of the earth? declare, if thou has understanding.

Who hath laid the measures thereof, if thou knowest? or who hath stretched the line upon it?...

By what way is the light parted, which scattereth the east wind upon the earth?

Who hath divided a watercourse for the overflowing of waters, or a way for the lightning of thunder?...

Out of whose womb came the ice? and the hoary frost of heaven, who hath gendered it?...

Knowest thou the ordinances of heaven? canst thou set the dominion thereof in the earth?

Canst thou lift up thy voice to the clouds, that abundance of waters may cover thee?...
Hast thou an arm like God? or canst thou thunder with a voice like him?
Doth the hawk fly by thy wisdom, and stretch her wings towards the south?
Canst thou draw out leviathan with a hook?

Asked to explain why Job has been made to suffer even though he has been good, God draws Job's attention to the mighty phenomena of nature. Do not be surprised that things have not gone your way, he declares: the universe is greater than you. Do not be surprised that you do not understand *why* they have not gone your way, for you cannot fathom the logic of the universe. See how small you are next to the mountains. Accept what is bigger than you and what you do not understand. The world may appear illogical to *you*, but it does not follow that it is illogical per se. Our lives are not the measure of all things: consider sublime places for a reminder of human insignificance and frailty.

There is a strictly religious message here. God assures Job that he has a place in his heart, even if all events do not centre around him and may at times appear to run contrary to his interest. When divine wisdom eludes human understanding, the righteous, made aware of their limitations by the spectacle of sublime nature, must continue to trust in God's plans for the universe.

8.

But the religious answer to Job's question does not invalidate the story for secular spirits. Sublime landscapes, through their grandeur and power, retain a symbolic role in bringing us to accept without bitterness or lamentation the obstacles that we cannot overcome and the events that we cannot make sense of. As the Old Testament God

knew, it can be helpful to back up deflationary points about mankind with reference to the very elements in nature which physically surpass it—the mountains, the girdle of the earth, the deserts.

If the world seems unfair or beyond our understanding, sublime places suggest that it is not surprising that things should be thus. We are the playthings of the forces that laid out the oceans and chiselled the mountains. Sublime places gently move us to acknowledge limitations that we might otherwise encounter with anxiety or anger in the ordinary flow of events. It is not just nature that defies us. Human life is as overwhelming. But it is the vast spaces of nature that perhaps provide us with the finest, the most respectful reminder of all that exceeds us. If we spend time in them, they may help us to accept more graciously the great, unfathomable events that molest our lives and will inevitably return us to dust.

ART

VII

On Eye-Opening Art

Place	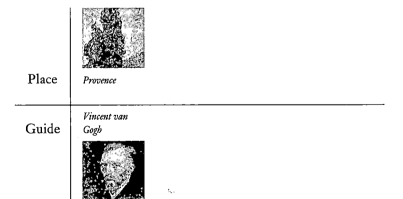*Provence*
Guide	*Vincent van Gogh*

1.

One summer I was invited to spend a few days with friends in a farmhouse in Provence. I knew that the word *Provence* was for many people rich in associations, though it meant little to me. I tended to switch off at its mention, out of a sense, founded on little, that the place would not be congenial to me. What I did know was that Provence was generally held by sensible people to be very beauti-ful—'Ah, Provence!' they would sigh, with a reverence otherwise reserved for opera or Delft porcelain.

I flew to Marseilles and, after renting a small Renault at the air-port, headed for the home of my hosts, which lay at the foot of the Alpilles hills, between the towns of Arles and Saint-Rémy. At the exit out of Marseilles, I grew confused and ended up at the giant oil refinery at Fos-sur-Mer, whose tangle of pipes and cooling towers spoke of the complexity involved in the manufacture of a liquid that I was used to putting into my car with scant thought for its origins.

I found my way back to the N568, which led me inland across the wheat-growing plain of La Crau. Outside the village of Saint-Martin-de-Crau, a few miles from my destination, being too early, I pulled off the road and turned off the engine. I had come to a stop on the edge of an olive grove. It was quiet save for the sounds made by cicadas hidden in the trees. Behind the grove were wheat fields bordered by a row of cypresses, over whose tops rose the irregular ridge of the Alpilles hills. The sky was a cloudless blue.

I scanned the view. I was not looking for anything in particular—not for predators, holiday homes or memories. My motive was sim-ple and hedonistic: I was looking for beauty. 'Delight and enliven me' was my implicit challenge to the olive trees, cypresses and skies of Provence. It was a vast, loose agenda, and my eyes were bewildered at their freedom. Without the motives that had marked the rest of the day—to seek out the airport, the exit out of Marseilles and so on—they careered from object to object, so that if their path had been traced by the mark of a giant pencil, the sky would soon have been darkened by random and impatient patterns.

Although the landscape was not ugly, I could not—after a few moments of scrutiny—detect the charm so often ascribed to it. The olive trees looked stunted, more like bushes than like trees, and the wheat fields evoked the flat, dull expanses of southeastern England, where I had attended a school and been unhappy. I lacked the energy to register the barns, the limestone of the hills or the poppies growing at the feet of a group of cypresses.

Bored and uncomfortable in the Renault's increasingly hot plastic interior, I set off for my destination and greeted my hosts with the remark that this was simply paradise.

Because we find places to be beautiful as immediately and as apparently spontaneously as we find snow to be cold or sugar sweet, it is hard to imagine that there is anything we might do to alter or expand our attractions. It seems that matters have been decided for us by qualities inherent in the places themselves or by hardwiring in our psyches, and that we would therefore be as helpless to modify our sense of the places we find beautiful as we would our preference for the ice creams we find appetising.

Yet aesthetic tastes may be less rigid than this analogy suggests. We overlook certain places because nothing has ever prompted us to conceive of them as being worthy of appreciation, or because some unfortunate but random association has turned us against them. Thus our relationship to olive trees might be improved if we directed our attention towards the silver in their leaves or the structure of their branches; new associations might be created around wheat once we are directed to the pathos of this fragile and yet essential crop as its stalks bend their grain-filled heads in the wind. We might find something to appreciate in the skies of Provence once we are told, even if only in the crudest way, that it is the shade of blue that counts.

And perhaps the most effective means of enriching our sense of what to look for in a scene is by studying visual art. We could conceive of many works of art as being immensely subtle instruments for telling us what amounts in effect to 'Look at the sky of Provence, redraw your notion of wheat, do justice to olive trees.' From amidst the million things in, for example, a wheat field, a successful work will draw out the features capable of exciting a sense of beauty and interest in the spectator. It will foreground elements ordinarily lost in the mass of data, stabilise them and, once we are acquainted with them, prompt us imperceptibly to find them in the world about us—or, if we have already found them, lend us the confidence to give them weight in our lives. We will be like a person around whom a word has been mentioned on many occasions, but who only begins to hear it once he or she has learnt its meaning.

And insofar as we travel in search of beauty, works of art may in small ways start to influence where we would like to travel *to*.

2.

Vincent van Gogh arrived in Provence at the end of February 1888. He was thirty-four years old and had dedicated himself to painting only eight years before, after failing in attempts to become first a teacher and then a priest. For the previous two years he had been living in Paris with his brother Theo, an art dealer, who supported him financially. He had had little artistic training but had befriended Paul Gauguin and Henri de Toulouse-Lautrec and exhibited his work alongside theirs at the Café du Tambourin on the Boulevard de Clichy.

'I can still remember vividly how excited I became that winter when travelling from Paris to Arles,' van Gogh would recall of his sixteen-hour train journey to Provence. On his arrival in what was then the most prosperous town in the region and a centre for the olive trade and railway engineering, van Gogh carried his bags in the snow (an exceptional ten inches had fallen that day) to the small Hotel Carrel, not far from Arles's northern ramparts. Despite the weather and the small size of his room, he was enthusiastic about his southerly move. As he told his sister, 'I believe that life here is just a little more satisfying than in many other spots.'

Van Gogh was to remain in Arles until May 1889, fifteen months during which he produced approximately two hundred paintings, a hundred drawings and two hundred letters—a period generally agreed to have been his greatest. The earliest works show Arles lying under snow, the sky a limpid blue, the earth a frozen pink. Five weeks after van Gogh arrived, spring came, and he painted fourteen canvases of trees in bloom in the fields outside the town. At the beginning of May he painted the Langlois drawbridge over the Arles-Bouc Canal, on the south side of Arles, and at the end of the month he produced a number of views from the plain of La Crau, looking towards the Alpilles hills and the ruined abbey of Montmajour. He also painted the reverse scene, climbing the rocky slopes of the abbey for a view of Arles. By the middle of June his attention had shifted to a new subject: the harvest, of which he completed ten paintings in only two weeks. He worked with extraordinary speed, or as he put it, 'quickly, quickly, quickly and in a hurry, like a harvester who is silent under the blazing sun, intent only on his reaping'. He noted, 'I work even in the middle of the day, in the full sunshine, and I enjoy it like a cicada. My God, if I had only known this part of the country at the age of twenty-five, instead of coming here when I was thirty-five years old!'

Later, explaining to his brother why he had moved from Paris to Arles, van Gogh offered two reasons: because he wanted to 'paint the South' and because he wanted, through his work, to help other people to 'see' it. However unsure he might be of his own powers to achieve that, he never wavered in his faith that the project was theoretically possible—that is, that artists could paint a portion of the world and in consequence open the eyes of others to it.

If he had such faith in the eye-opening power of art, it was because he had often experienced it himself, as a spectator. Since moving to France from his native Holland, he had felt it most particularly in relation to literature. He had read the works of Balzac, Flaubert, Zola and Maupassant and been grateful to those writers for opening his eyes to the dynamics of French society and psychology. *Madame Bovary* had taught him about provincial middle-class life, and *Père Goriot* about penniless but ambitious students in Paris; he now recognised the characters from these novels in society at large.

Paintings had similarly opened his eyes. Van Gogh frequently paid tribute to painters who had allowed him to see certain colours and atmospheres. Velázquez, for example, had given him a map that allowed him to see grey. Several of Velázquez's canvases depicted humble Iberian interiors with walls of brick or a sombre plaster, where, even in the middle of the day, when the shutters were closed to protect the house from the heat, the dominant colour was a sepulchral grey, occasionally pierced, where the shutters were not quite closed or where a section had been chipped off them, by a shaft of brilliant yellow. Velázquez had not invented such effects; many others must have seen them before him, but few had had the energy or the talent to capture them and transform them into communicable experience. Like an explorer with a new continent, Velázquez had, for van Gogh at least, given his name to a discovery in the world of light.

Van Gogh ate in many small restaurants in the centre of Arles. Their walls were often dark, and the shutters closed against the bright sunlight outside. One lunchtime, he wrote to his brother to announce that he had stumbled upon something utterly Velázquezian: 'The restaurant in which I am sitting is very strange. It is grey all over... a Velázquez grey—as in the *Spinning Women*—and there is even a very narrow, very fierce ray of sunlight coming through a blind, just like the one that slants across Velázquez's picture.... In the kitchen are an old woman and a short, fat servant also in grey, black, white... it's pure Velázquez.'

It was for van Gogh the mark of every great painter to enable viewers to see certain aspects of the world more clearly. If Velázquez was his guide to grey and to the coarse faces of large cooks, then Monet was his guide to sunsets, Rembrandt to morning light and Vermeer to adolescent girls ('A perfect Vermeer,' he exclaimed to Theo after he spotted one example near the arena). The sky over the Rhône after a heavy rain shower reminded him of Hokusai, the wheat of Millet and the young women in Saintes-Maries de la Mer of Cimabue and Giotto.

3.

Nevertheless—and fortunately for his artistic ambitions—van Gogh did not believe that previous artists had captured everything there was to see in southern France. To the contrary, many had, in his view, completely missed the essentials. 'Good Lord, I have seen things by certain painters that did not do justice to the subject at all,' he exclaimed. 'There is plenty for me to work on here.'

No one had, for example, captured the distinctive appearance of the middle-aged middle-class women of Arles, of whom van Gogh asserted, 'Some women resemble a Fragonard and some a Renoir, but there are others who *cannot be labelled according to anything that has ever yet been done in painting*' (emphasis added). The farm labourers whom he saw working in the fields outside of Arles had likewise been ignored by artists: 'Millet has reawakened our minds so that we can see the dweller in nature. But until now no one has painted the real *southern* Frenchman for us.' He elaborated, 'Have we in general learned to see the peasant now? *No;* hardly anyone knows how to pull that off.'

The Provence that greeted van Gogh in 1888 had already been the subject of painting for over a hundred years. Among the better-known Provençal artists were Fragonard (1732–1806), Constantin (1756–1844), Bidauld (1758–1846), Granet (1775–1849) and Aiguier (1814–1865). All were realistic painters, adhering to the classical and until then relatively undisputed notion that their task was to render on canvas an accurate version of the visual world. They went out into the fields and mountains of Provence and painted recognisable versions of cypresses, trees, grass, wheat, clouds and bulls.

Yet van Gogh insisted that most had failed to do justice to their subjects. They had not, he claimed, produced realistic depictions of Provence. We are apt to call any painting realistic that competently conveys key elements of the world. But the world is complex enough for two realistic pictures of the same place, at the same moment, to look very different, as a consequence of differences in artistic styles and temperaments. Two realistic artists may sit at the edge of the same olive grove and produce divergent sketches. Every realistic picture represents a choice as to which features of reality should be given prominence; no painting ever captures the whole, as Nietzsche mockingly pointed out in a bit of doggerel verse entitled 'The Realistic Painter':

> *'Completely true to nature!'—what a lie:*
> *How could nature ever be constrained into a picture?*
> *The smallest bit of nature is infinite!*
> *And so he paints what he likes about it.*
> *And what does he like? He likes what he can paint!*

If we in turn like a painter's work, it is perhaps because we judge that he or she has selected the features that we believe to be the most valuable within a particular scene. There are selections so acute that they come to define a place, with the result that we can no longer travel through that landscape without being reminded of what a great artist noticed there.

Alternatively, if we complain that, for example, our portrait does not look 'like us', we are not accusing its painter of trickery; we are simply suggesting that the process of selection that goes on in any work of art has in this instance gone wrong, and that parts of us that we think of as belonging to our essential selves have not been given their due. Bad art might thus be defined as a series of bad choices about what to show and what to leave out.

And leaving out the essential was precisely what van Gogh accused most of the artists who had painted southern France before him of doing.

4.

There was a large book on him in the guest bedroom, and because I was unable to sleep on my first night, I read several chapters, eventually falling asleep with the volume open on my lap as a trace of dawn-red appeared in the corner of the window.

I awoke late and found that my hosts had gone to Saint-Rémy, leaving a note to say that they would be back around lunchtime. Breakfast was laid out on a metal table on the terrace, and I ate three *pains au chocolat* in guilty, rapid succession, all the while keeping one eye out for the housekeeper, who I feared might put an unflattering spin on my gourmandise for her employers.

It was a clear day, with a mistral blowing that ruffled the heads of the wheat in an adjacent field. I had sat in this same spot the day before, but only now did I notice that there were two large cypresses growing at the end of the garden, a discovery that was not unconnected to the chapter I had read the night before on van Gogh's treatment of the tree. He had sketched a series of cypresses in 1888 and 1889. 'They are constantly occupying my thoughts,' he told his brother. 'It astonishes me that they have not yet been done as I see them. The cypress is as beautiful in line and proportion as an Egyptian obelisk. And the green has a quality of such distinction. It is a splash of *black* in a sunny landscape, but it is one of the most interesting black notes, and the most difficult to get exactly right.'

What did van Gogh notice about cypresses that others had failed to see? In part, the way they moved in the wind. I walked to the end of the garden and there studied, thanks to certain works (*Cypresses* and *Wheat Field with Cypresses* of 1889 in particular), their distinctive behaviour in the mistral.

Vincent van Gogh, *Cypresses*, 1889

Vincent van Gogh, *Wheat Field with Cypresses,* 1889

There are architectural reasons for this movement. Unlike pine branches, which descend gently downwards from the top of their tree, the fronds of the cypress thrust upwards from the ground. The cypress's trunk is, moreover, unusually short, with the top third of the tree being made up wholly of branches. Whereas an oak will shake its branches but keep its trunk immobile in the wind, the cypress will bend, and furthermore, because of the way the fronds grow from a number of points along the circumference of the trunk, it will seem to bend along different axes. From a distance, the lack of synchronicity in its movements makes it look as though the cypress were being shifted by several gusts of wind blowing from different angles. With its conelike shape (cypresses rarely exceed a metre in diameter), the tree takes on the appearance of a flame flickering nervously in the wind. All of this van Gogh noticed and would make others see.

A few years after van Gogh's stay in Provence, Oscar Wilde remarked that there had been no fog in London before Whistler painted it. Surely, too, there were fewer cypresses in Provence before van Gogh painted *them*.

Olive trees must also have been less noticeable. I had the previous day dismissed one example as a squat, bushlike thing, but in *Olive Trees with Yellow Sky and Sun* and *Olive Grove: Orange Sky* of 1889, van Gogh brought out (that is, foregrounded) the shape of the olives' trunks and leaves.

I now noted an angularity that I had earlier missed: the trees resemble tridents that have been flung from a great height into the soil. There is a ferocity to the olive trees' branches, too, as if they were flexed arms ready to hit out. And whereas the leaves of many other trees make one think of limp lettuce emptied over racks of naked branches, the taut, silvery olive leaves give an impression of alertness and contained energy.

After van Gogh, I began to notice that there was something unusual about the colours of Provence as well. There are climatic reasons for this. The mistral, blowing along the Rhône Valley from the Alps, regularly clears the sky of clouds and moisture, leaving it a pure, rich blue without a trace of white. At the same time, a high water table and good irrigation promote a plant life of singular lushness for a Mediterranean climate. With no water shortages to restrict its growth, the vegetation draws full benefit from the great advantages of the South: light and heat. And fortuitously, because there is no moisture in the air, there is in Provence, unlike the tropics, no mistiness to dampen and meld the colours of the trees, flowers and plants. The combination of a cloudless sky, dry air, water and rich vegetation leaves the region dominated by vivid primary, contrasting colours.

Painters before van Gogh had tended to ignore these contrasts and to paint only in complementary colours, as Claude and Poussin had taught them to do. Constantin and Bidauld, for example, had depicted Provence entirely in subtle gradations of soft blue and brown. Van Gogh was incensed by this neglect of the landscape's natural colour scheme: 'The majority of [painters], because they aren't colourists...do not see yellow, orange or sulphur in the South, and they call a painter mad if he sees with eyes other than theirs.' He abandoned their chiaroscuro technique and soaked his canvases in primary colours, always arranging them in such a way that their contrast would be maximised: red with green, yellow with purple, blue with orange. 'The colour is exquisite here,' he wrote to his sister. 'When the green leaves are fresh, it is a rich green, the likes of which we seldom see in the North. Even when it gets scorched and dusty, the landscape does not lose its beauty, for then it takes on tones of gold of various tints: green-gold, yellow-gold, pink-

Vincent van Gogh, *Olive Grove: Orange Sky,* 1889

gold...And this [is then] combined with blue, from the deepest royal blue of the water to the blue of the forget-me-nots, a cobalt, particularly clear bright blue.'

My own eyes grew attuned to see around me the colours that had dominated van Gogh's canvases. Everywhere I looked, I could see primary colours in contrast. Beside the house was a violet-coloured field of lavender next to a yellow field of wheat. The roofs of the buildings were orange against a pure blue sky. Green meadows were dotted with red poppies and bordered by oleanders.

It is not only the day that abounds in colours in Provence; van Gogh saw that and brought out the colours of the night as well. Previous Provençal painters had depicted the night sky as groupings of little white dots against a dark background. But when one sits under the Provençal sky on a clear night far from the glow of houses and street lamps, one notices that the sky in fact contains a profusion of colours: between the stars, it seems a deep blue, violet or very dark green, whereas the stars themselves appear to be a pale yellow, orange or green, diffusing rings of light far beyond their own narrow circumference. As van Gogh explained to his sister, 'The night is even more richly coloured than the day.... If only one pays attention to it, one sees that certain stars are citron yellow, while others have a pink glow or a green, blue and forget-me-not brilliance. And without my expiating on this theme, it should be clear that putting little white dots on a blue-black surface is not enough.'

5.
The tourist office in Arles is housed in an undistinguished concrete block in the southwestern part of town. It offers visitors the usual fare: free maps, advice on hotels and information about cultural festivals, child-minders, wine tastings, canoeing, ruins and markets.

One attraction is emphasised above all others: 'Welcome to the land of Vincent van Gogh,' exclaims a poster with the sunflowers in the entrance hall; inside, the walls are decorated with harvest scenes, olive trees and orchards.

The office particularly recommends what it describes as the 'van Gogh trail'. On the one hundredth anniversary of his death in 1890, van Gogh's presence in Provence was honoured by a series of plaques—fixed onto metal rods or stone slabs—positioned in some of the places he painted. The plaques feature photographs of the relevant works and a few lines of commentary. They are to be found both within the town and in the wheat and olive fields that surround it. They extend as far as Saint-Rémy, where, after the ear incident, van Gogh ended his Provençal days at the Maison de Santé.

I persuaded my hosts to spend an afternoon following the trail, to which end we stopped in at the tourist office to collect a map. By chance we learnt that a guided tour, a once-weekly event, was about to start in the courtyard outside, and that there were still places available for a modest sum. We joined a dozen other enthusiasts and were first taken to the Place Lamartine by a guide, who told us that her name was Sophie and that she was writing a thesis on van Gogh at the Sorbonne in Paris.

At the beginning of May 1888, finding his hotel too expensive, van Gogh had rented a wing of a building at 2 Place Lamartine known as the Yellow House. It was one half of a double-fronted building that had been painted bright yellow by its owner but left unfinished inside. Van Gogh developed a great interest in the interior design. He wanted it to be solid and simple, painted in the colours of the South: red, green, blue, orange, sulphur and lilac. 'I want to make it really *an artist's house*—nothing *precious,* but with everything from the chairs to the pictures having character,' he told his brother. 'About

Vincent van Gogh, *'The Yellow House' (Vincent's House), Arles,* 1888

the beds, I have bought country beds, big double ones instead of iron ones. That gives an appearance of solidity, durability and quiet.' The refurbishment complete, he wrote elatedly to his sister, 'My house here is painted the yellow colour of fresh butter on the outside, with glaringly green shutters; it stands in the full sunlight in a square that has a green garden with plane trees, oleanders and acacias. It is completely whitewashed inside, with a floor made of red bricks. And over it there is the intensely blue sky. In this house I can live and breathe, meditate and paint.'

Sadly, Sophie had little to show us, for the Yellow House had been destroyed in the Second World War and subsequently replaced with a student hostel, which itself was now dwarfed by the giant Monoprix supermarket that had gone up beside it. We drove next to Saint-Rémy and there spent more than an hour in the fields around the asylum where van Gogh had lived and painted. Sophie had with her a large plastic-coated book containing the main Provence paintings, and she frequently held it up in spots where van Gogh had worked, letting the rest of us crowd around to look on. At one point, with her back to the Alpilles, she held up *Olive Trees with the Alpilles in the Background* (June 1889), and we admired both the view and van Gogh's version of it.

But there was a moment of dissent in the group. Next to me, an Australian wearing a large hat said to his companion, a small, tousle-haired woman, 'Well, it doesn't look much like that.'

Van Gogh himself had feared he might encounter such accusations. To his sister, he wrote that many people already said of his work, ' "This really looks too strange," not to mention those who think it a total abortion and utterly repulsive.' The reasons for such opinions were not hard to find: the walls of his houses were not always straight, the sun was not always yellow or the grass green, there was an exaggerated sense of movement in some of his trees. 'I have played hell somewhat with the truthfulness of the colours,' he admitted, and he played similar hell with proportion, line, shadow and tone.

Yet in playing hell, van Gogh was only making more explicit a process in which all artists are involved—namely, choosing which aspects of reality to include in a work and which to leave out. As Nietzsche knew, reality itself is infinite and can never be wholly represented in art. What made van Gogh unusual among Provençal artists was his choice of what he felt was important. Whereas painters such as Constantin had expended much effort in getting the scale right, van Gogh, though passionately interested in producing a 'likeness', insisted that it was not by worrying about scale that he would end up conveying what was important in the South: his art would involve, as he mockingly told his brother, 'a likeness different from the products of the God-fearing photographer'. The part of reality that concerned him sometimes required distortion, omission and the substitution of colours to be brought to the fore, but it was still the real—the 'likeness'—that interested him. He was willing to sacrifice a naive realism in order to achieve realism of a deeper sort, like a poet who, though less factual than a journalist in describing an event, may nevertheless reveal truths about it that find no place in the other's literal grid.

Van Gogh elaborated on this idea in a letter he wrote to his brother in September 1888 about a portrait he was planning: 'Rather than trying to reproduce exactly what I see before my eyes, I use colour more arbitrarily, in order to express myself forcibly.... I'll give you an example of what I mean: I should like to paint the portrait of an artist friend, a man who dreams great dreams, who works as the nightingale sings, because it is his nature [the portrait was *Poet*, of

The van Gogh Trail, Saint-Rémy-de-Provence

early September 1888]. He'll be blond. *I want to put my appreciation, the love I have for him, into the picture.* So I paint him as he is, as faithfully as I can, to begin with. But the picture is not yet finished. In order to finish it, I am going to be the arbitrary colourist. I mean to exaggerate the fairness of the hair, even get to orange tones, chromes and pale citron yellow. Behind the head, instead of painting the ordinary wall of the mean room, I will paint infinity, a plain background of the richest, most intense blue I can contrive, and by this simple combination of the bright head against the rich blue background, I will achieve a mysterious effect, like a star in the depths of an azure sky.... Oh, my dear boy...and the nice people will see the exaggeration only as a caricature.' [*Emphasis added*]

A few weeks later, van Gogh began another 'caricature'. 'Tonight I am probably going to start on the interior of the café where I eat, by gaslight, in the evening,' he told his brother. 'It is what they call a *café de nuit* (these are fairly common here), one that stays open all night. Night prowlers can take refuge there when they have no money to pay for a lodging or are too drunk to be taken in elsewhere.' In painting what would become *The Night Café in Arles,* van Gogh abandoned adherence to some elements of 'reality' for the sake of others. He did not reproduce the proper perspective or colour scheme of the café; his light bulbs metamorphosed into glowing mushrooms, his chairs arched their backs, his floor buckled. Yet he was still interested in expressing truthful ideas about the place, ideas that would perhaps have been less well expressed if he had had to follow the classical rules of art.

6.

The complaints of the Australian man were unusual within our group; most of the rest of us came away from Sophie's lecture with a newfound reverence both for van Gogh and for the landscapes he painted. But my own enthusiasm was undermined by the memory of an exceptionally acerbic maxim that Pascal had penned several centuries before van Gogh's southern journey: 'How vain painting is, exciting admiration by its resemblance to things of which we do not admire the originals' (*Pensées*, 40).

It struck me as awkwardly true that I had not much admired Provence before I began to study its depiction in van Gogh's work. But in its desire to mock art lovers, Pascal's maxim was in danger of skirting two important points. Admiring a painting that depicts a place we know but don't like seems absurd and pretentious if we imagine that painters do nothing but reproduce exactly what lies before them. If that were true, then all we could admire in a painting would be the technical skills involved in the reproduction of an object and the glamorous name of the painter, in which case we would have little difficulty agreeing with Pascal's description of painting as a vain pursuit. But as Nietzsche knew, painters do *not* merely reproduce; they select and highlight, and they are accorded genuine admiration insofar as their version of reality seems to bring out valuable features of it.

Furthermore, we do not have to resume our indifference to a place once the painting of it that we have admired is out of sight, as Pascal hints. Our capacity to appreciate can be transferred from art to the world. We can find things that delight us on a canvas first but then later welcome them in the place where the canvas was painted. We can continue to see cypresses beyond van Gogh's paintings.

7.
Provence is not the only place that I began to appreciate and wanted to explore because of its portrayal in art. I once visited Germany's

industrial zones because of Wim Wenders's *Alice in the Cities*. The photographs of Andreas Gursky gave me a taste for the undersides of motorway bridges. Patrick Keiller's documentary *Robinson in Space* made me take a holiday around the factories, shopping malls and business parks of southern England.

In recognising that a landscape can become more attractive to us once we have seen it through the eyes of a great artist, the tourist office in Arles is only exploiting a long-standing relationship between art and the desire to travel, a connection evident in different countries (and in different artistic media) throughout the history of tourism. Perhaps the most notable and earliest example emerged in Britain in the second half of the eighteenth century.

Historians contend that large parts of the countryside of England, Scotland and Wales went unappreciated before the eighteenth century. Places that were later taken to be naturally and inarguably beautiful—the Wye Valley, the Highlands of Scotland, the Lake District—were for centuries treated with indifference, even disdain. Daniel Defoe, for example, travelling in the Lake District in the 1720s, described it as 'barren and frightful'. In his *Journey to the Western Isles of Scotland*, Dr Johnson wrote that the Highlands, 'rough' and pitifully devoid of 'vegetable decoration', were 'a wide extent of hopeless sterility'. When, at Glenshiel, Boswell attempted to cheer him up by pointing out that a mountain seemed impressively high, Johnson snapped irritably, 'No; it is no more than a considerable protuberance.'

At that time, those who could afford to travel went abroad. Italy was the most popular destination, and especially Rome, Naples and the surrounding countryside. It was perhaps no coincidence that these locales were prominently featured in the very works of art most favoured by the British aristocracy: the poetry of Virgil and

Horace and the paintings of Poussin and Claude. The paintings depicted the Roman exurbs and the Neapolitan coastline. It was often dawn or dusk, with a few fleecy clouds floating overhead, their borders pink and golden. One imagined that it was going to be, or had been, a very hot day. The air seemed quiet, the silence interrupted only by the flow of a refreshing brook or the sound of oars cutting through a lake. A few shepherdesses might be gamboling through a field or looking after some sheep or a golden-haired child. Gazing at such scenes in English country houses in the rain, many would have dreamt of crossing the Channel at the earliest available opportunity. As Joseph Addison observed in 1712, 'We find the Works of Nature still more pleasant, the more they resemble those of Art.'

Unfortunately for the works of British nature, for a long time few works of art resembled them at all. Yet during the eighteenth century this dearth was gradually overcome, and so, too, with uncanny synchronicity, was the reluctance of the British to travel around their own islands. In 1727, the poet James Thomson published *The Seasons*, which celebrated the agricultural life and landscape of southern England. Its success helped to bring to prominence the work of other 'ploughmen poets', including Stephen Duck, Robert Burns and John Clare. British painters began to consider their country, too. Lord Shelburne commissioned Thomas Gainsborough and George Barrett to paint a series of landscapes for his Wiltshire house, Bowood, declaring his intention 'to lay the foundation of a school of British landscape'. Richard Wilson went to paint the Thames near Twickenham, Thomas Hearne depicted Goodrich Castle, Philip de Loutherbourg painted Tintern Abbey, and Thomas Smith portrayed Derwentwater and Windermere.

No sooner had the process begun than there was an explosion in the number of people travelling around the isles. For the first time,

Vincent van Gogh, *Sunset: Wheat Fields near Arles*, 1888

the Wye Valley was filled with tourists, as were the mountains of North Wales, the Lake District and the Scottish Highlands, a trend that seems perfectly to confirm the contention that we tend to seek out corners of the world only after they have been painted and written about by artists.

The theory must of course be a sharp exaggeration, as sharp as the suggestion that no one paid any attention to fog in London before Whistler or to cypresses in Provence before van Gogh. Art cannot single-handedly create enthusiasm, nor does it arise from sentiments of which nonartists are devoid; it merely contributes to enthusiasm and guides us to be more conscious of feelings that we might previously have experienced only tentatively or hurriedly.

But that may—as the tourist office in Arles seemed to understand—be enough to influence where we choose to go next year.

VIII

On Possessing Beauty

The Lake District

| Places | *Madrid* | *Amsterdam* | *Barbados* | *London Docklands* |

| Guide | *John Ruskin* |

1.

Among all the places that we go to but don't look at properly or that leave us indifferent, a few occasionally stand out with an impact that overwhelms us and forces us to take heed. They possess a quality that might clumsily be called beauty. This may not involve prettiness nor any of the obvious features that guidebooks associate with beauty spots; having recourse to the word might be just another way of saying that we like a place.

There was much beauty on my travels. In Madrid, a few blocks from my hotel, there lay a patch of waste ground bordered by apartment buildings and a large, orange-coloured petrol station with a carwash. One evening, in the darkness, a long, sleek, almost empty train passed several metres above the roof of the station and wended its way amongst the apartment buildings, on a level with their middle floors. With its viaduct lost in the night, the train appeared to float above the earth, a technological feat that looked more plausible given the train's futuristic shape and the pale ghostly-green light emanating from its windows. Inside the apartments, people were watching television or moving around their kitchens; meanwhile, dispersed through the carriages, the few passengers stared out at the city or read newspapers: the start of a journey to Seville or Córdoba that would end long after the dishwashers had reached the end of their cycles and the televisions fallen silent. The passengers and apartment dwellers paid little attention to one another; their lives ran along lines that would never meet, except for a brief moment in the retina of an observer who had taken a walk to escape a sad hotel room.

In Amsterdam, in a courtyard behind a wooden door, there was an old brick wall that despite a tear-inducing wind blowing along the canals had slowly heated itself up in a fragile early-spring sun. I took my hands from my pockets and ran them along the bricks' gnarled and pitted surface. They seemed light and ready to crumble. I felt the impulse to kiss them, so as to experience more closely a texture that reminded me of blocks of pumice or halva from a Lebanese delicatessen.

In Barbados, on the eastern shore, I looked out across a dark-violet sea that stretched unhindered to the coasts of Africa. The island suddenly seemed small and vulnerable, its theatrical vegetation of wild pink flowers and shaggy trees a touching protest against the sober monotony of the sea. In the Lake District, I took in the view at dawn from our window in the Mortal Man: hills of soft Silurian rock covered in fine green grass above which a layer of mist was hovering. The hills undulated as though they formed part of the backbone of a giant beast that had lain down to sleep and might at any point awake and stand up several miles high, shaking off oak trees and hedgerows like pieces of fluff caught on its green felt jacket.

2.

A dominant impulse on encountering beauty is to wish to hold on to it, to possess it and give it weight in one's life. There is an urge to say, 'I was here, I saw this and it mattered to me.'

But beauty is fugitive, being frequently found in places to which we may never return or else resulting from rare conjunctions of season, light and weather. How then to possess it, how to hold on to the floating train, the halvalike bricks or the English valley?

The camera provides one option. Taking photographs can assuage the itch for possession sparked by the beauty of a place; our anxiety over losing a precious scene can decline with every click of the shutter. Or else we can try to imprint ourselves physically on a place of beauty, perhaps hoping to render it more present in us by making *ourselves* more present in *it*. In Alexandria, standing before Pompey's Pillar, we could try to carve our name in the granite, to follow the example of Flaubert's friend Thompson from Sunderland. ('You can't see the pillar without seeing Thompson's name, and consequently thinking of Thompson. This cretin has thus become part of the monument and has perpetuated himself along with it.... All imbeciles are more or less Thompsons from Sunderland.') A more modest step might be to buy something—a bowl, a lacquered box or a pair of sandals (Flaubert acquired three carpets in Cairo)— as a reminder of what we have lost, like a lock of hair cut from a departing lover's mane.

3.

John Ruskin was born in London in February 1819. A central part of his work was to pivot around the question of how we can possess the beauty of places.

From an early age, he was unusually alive to the smallest features of the visual world. He recalled that at three or four, 'I could pass my days contentedly in tracing the squares and comparing the colours of my carpet—examining the knots in the wood of the floor, or counting the bricks in the opposite houses with rapturous intervals of excitement.' Ruskin's parents encouraged his sensitivity. His mother introduced him to nature, while his father, a prosperous sherry importer, read the classics to him after tea and took him to a museum every Saturday. Over the summer holidays, the family travelled around the British Isles and mainland Europe, not for entertainment or diversion but for beauty, by which they meant chiefly the beauty of the Alps and of the medieval cities of northern France and Italy, in particular Amiens and Venice. They journeyed slowly, in a carriage, never covering more than twenty-five miles a day, and stopping every few miles to admire the scenery—a way of travelling that Ruskin was to practise throughout his life.

Ruskin's interest in beauty and in its possession led him to five central conclusions. First, beauty was the result of a number of complex factors that affected the mind both psychologically and visually. Second, humans had an innate tendency to respond to beauty and to desire to possess it. Third, there were many lower expressions of this desire for possession (including, as we have seen, buying souvenirs and carpets, carving one's name on a pillar and taking photographs). Fourth, there was only one way to possess beauty properly, and that was by *understanding* it, by making oneself conscious of the factors (psychological and visual) responsible for it. And last, the most effective means of pursuing this conscious understanding was by attempting to describe beautiful places through art, by writing about or drawing them, irrespective of whether one happened to have any talent for doing so.

4.

Between 1856 and 1860, Ruskin's primary intellectual concern consisted in teaching people how to draw. 'The art of drawing,' he maintained, 'which is of more real importance to the human race than that of writing and should be taught to every child just as writing is, has been so neglected and abused, that there is not one man in a thousand, even of its professed teachers, who knows its first principles.'

To begin rectifying the situation, Ruskin published two books, *The Elements of Drawing* (1857) and *The Elements of Perspective* (1859), and gave a series of lectures at the Working Men's College in London, where he instructed students—mostly Cockney craftsmen—in techniques of shading, colour, dimension, perspective and framing. The lectures were heavily subscribed, and the books were critical and commercial successes, confirming Ruskin in his view that drawing should not be for the few: 'There is a satisfactory and available power in every one to learn drawing if he wishes, just as nearly all persons have the power of learning French, Latin or arithmetic, in a decent and useful degree.'

What was the point of drawing? Ruskin saw no paradox in stressing that it had nothing to do with drawing *well* or with becoming an artist: 'A man is born an artist as a hippopotamus is born a hippopotamus; and you can no more *make* yourself one than you can make yourself a giraffe.' He did not mind if his East End students left his classes unable to draw anything that would ever be hung in a gallery. 'My efforts are directed not to making a carpenter an artist, but to making him happier as a carpenter,' he told a royal commission on drawing in 1857. He explained that he himself was far from being a talented artist. Of his own childhood drawings, he said mockingly, 'I never saw any boy's work in my life showing so little original faculty, or grasp by memory. I could literally draw nothing, not a cat, not a mouse, not a boat, not a brush.'

If drawing had value even when practised by those with no talent, it was, Ruskin believed, because it could teach us to see—that is, to notice rather than merely look. In the process of re-creating with our own hands what lies before our eyes, we seem naturally to evolve from observing beauty in a loose way to possessing a deep understanding of its constituent parts and hence more secure memories of it. A tradesman who had studied at the Working Men's College reported what Ruskin told him and his fellow students at the end of their course: ' "Now, remember, gentlemen, that I have not been trying to teach you to draw, only to *see*. Two men are walking through Clare Market. One of them comes out at the other end not a bit wiser than when he went in; the other notices a bit of parsley hanging over the edge of a butter-woman's basket, and carries away with him images of beauty which in the course of his daily work he incorporates with it for many a day. I want you to see things like these." '

Ruskin was distressed by how seldom people noticed details. He deplored the blindness and haste of modern tourists, especially those who prided themselves on covering Europe in a week by train (a service first offered by Thomas Cook in 1862): 'No changing of place at a hundred miles an hour will make us one whit stronger, happier, or wiser. There was always more in the world than men could see, walked they ever so slowly; they will see it no better for going fast. The really precious things are thought and sight, not pace. It does a bullet no good to go fast; and a man, if he be truly a man, no harm to go slow; for his glory is not at all in going, but in being.'

It is a measure of how accustomed we are to inattention that we would be thought unusual and perhaps dangerous if we stopped and stared at a place for as long as a sketcher would require to draw it. Ten minutes of acute concentration at least are needed to draw a tree, but even the prettiest tree rarely detains passersby for longer than a minute.

Ruskin connected the wish to travel fast and far with the inability to derive appropriate pleasure from any one place or, by extension, from details such as single sprigs of parsley hanging over the edges of baskets. In a moment of particular frustration with the tourist industry, he harangued an audience of wealthy industrialists in Manchester in 1864, charging, 'Your one conception of pleasure is to drive in railroad carriages. You have put a railroad bridge over the fall of Schaffenhausen. You have tunnelled the cliffs of Lucerne by Tell's chapel; you have destroyed the Clarens shore of the Lake of Geneva; there is not a quiet valley in England that you have not filled with bellowing fire nor any foreign city in which the spread of your presence is not marked by a consuming white leprosy of new hotels. The Alps themselves you look upon as soaped poles in a bear-garden, which you set yourselves to climb, and slide down again, with "shrieks of delight".'

The tone was hysterical, but the dilemma was genuine. Technology may make it easier to reach beauty, but it does not simplify the process of possessing or appreciating it.

What, then, was wrong with photography? Nothing, thought Ruskin initially. 'Among all the mechanical poison that this terrible nineteenth century has poured upon men, it has given us at any rate *one* antidote,' he wrote of Louis-Jacques-Mandé Daguerre's invention of 1839. In Venice in 1845, he made numerous daguerreotypes and delighted in the results. To his father he wrote, 'Daguerreotypes taken by this vivid sunlight are glorious things. It is very nearly the same thing as carrying off a palace itself—every chip of stone and stain is there—and of course, there can be no mistakes about proportion.'

Yet Ruskin's enthusiasm diminished as he began to note the devilish problem that photography created for the majority of its practitioners. Rather than employing it as a supplement to active, conscious seeing, they used the medium as a substitute, paying *less* attention to the world than they had done previously, taking it on faith that photography automatically assured them possession of it.

In explaining his love of drawing (it was rare for him to travel anywhere without sketching something), Ruskin once remarked that it had arisen not from a desire 'for reputation, [or] for the good of others, [or] for my own advantage, but from a sort of instinct *like that of eating or drinking*'. What unites the three activities is that they all involve assimilations by the self of desirable elements from the world, a transfer of goodness from without to within. As a child, Ruskin said, he had so loved the look of grass that he had frequently wanted to eat it, but gradually he had discovered that it would be better to try to draw it: 'I used to lie down on it and draw the blades as they grew—until every square foot of meadow, or mossy bank, became a *possession* to me' (emphasis added).

Photography alone could not, and cannot, ensure such eating. True possession of a scene is a matter of making a conscious effort to notice elements and understand their construction. We can see beauty well enough just by opening our eyes, but how long this beauty will survive in memory depends on how intentionally we have apprehended it. The camera blurs the distinction between looking and noticing, between seeing and possessing; it may give us the option of true knowledge, but it may also unwittingly make the effort of acquiring that knowledge seem superfluous. It suggests that we have done all the work simply by taking a photograph, whereas proper eating of a place—a woodland, for example—requires that we pose ourselves a series of questions such as 'How do the stems connect to the roots?' 'Where is the mist coming from?' 'Why does one tree seem darker than another?' These questions are implicitly asked and answered in the process of sketching.

5.

Encouraged by Ruskin's democratic vision of drawing, I tried my hand at it during my travels. As to what I should draw, it seemed sensible to be guided by the same desire to possess beauty that had previously led me to take up my camera. In Ruskin's words, 'Your art is

John Ruskin, *Study of a Peacock's Breast Feather*, 1873

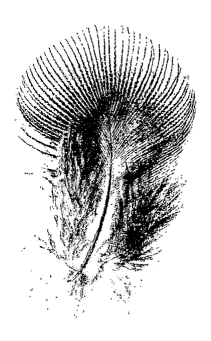

to be the praise of something that you love. It may only be the praise of a shell or a stone.'

I decided to draw the bedroom window at the Mortal Man because it was to hand and seemed attractive on a bright autumn morning. The result was a predictable yet instructive disaster. The very act of drawing an object, however badly, swiftly takes the drawer from a woolly sense of what the object looks like to a precise awareness of its component parts and particularities. 'A window' thus reveals itself to be made up of a succession of ledges holding the glass in place, a system of ridges and indentations (the hotel was in the Georgian style), twelve panes that at a glance seem square but are in fact mildly though importantly rectangular, and white paint that is not really white but rather ash-grey, brown-grey, yellow, pinky-mauve or mild green depending on the light and on the relationship between the light and the condition of the underlying wood (in the northwestern edge of the window, for example, a trace of damp gave the paint a pinky tint). Nor, as it turns out, is glass wholly clear, having within it minute imperfections, tiny bubbles of air like those in a frozen fizzy drink; on its surface, moreover, mine was marked with the traces of dried raindrops and the impatient swipes of a window cleaner's cloth.

Drawing brutally shows up our previous blindness to the true appearance of things. Consider the case of trees. In a passage in *The Elements of Drawing*, Ruskin discussed, with reference to his own illustrations, the difference between the way we usually imagine the branches of trees before we draw them and the way they reveal themselves once we have looked more closely with the help of a pad and pencil: 'The stem does not merely send off a wild branch here and there to take its own way, but all the branches share in one great fountain-like impulse. That is to say, the general type of a tree is not

John Ruskin, *Velvet Crab, c.* 1870–71

as 1a but as 1b, in which the boughs all carry their minor divisions right out to the bounding curve. And the type of each separate bough is not 2a but 2b; approximating, that is to say, to the structure of a plant of broccoli.'

John Ruskin, *Branches*, from his *Elements of Drawing*, 1857

I had seen many oak trees in my life, but only after an hour spent drawing one in the Langdale Valley (the result would have shamed an infant) did I begin to appreciate, and remember, their identity.

6.

Another benefit we may derive from drawing is a conscious understanding of the reasons behind our attraction to certain landscapes and buildings. Through drawing, we may find explanations for our tastes and begin to develop an 'aesthetic', or a capacity to assert judgements about beauty and ugliness. We may determine with greater precision what is missing from a building we don't like and what contributes to the beauty of one we do. We may be able more quickly to analyse a scene that impresses us and to pin down whence its power arises ('the combination of limestone and evening sun', 'the way the trees taper down to the river'). We may move from a numb 'I like this' to a more exacting 'I like this because...', and then in turn towards a generalisation about the likeable. Even if they are held only in exploratory, tentative ways, laws of beauty come to mind: it is better for light to strike objects from the side than from overhead; grey goes well with green; in order for a street to convey a sense of space, the buildings must be no taller than the street is wide.

And on the basis of this conscious awareness, more solid memories can be founded. Carving our name on Pompey's Pillar begins to seem unnecessary. Drawing allows us, in Ruskin's account, 'to stay the cloud in its fading, the leaf in its trembling, and the shadows in their changing'.

Summing up what he had attempted to do in four years of teaching and writing manuals on drawing, Ruskin explained that he had been motivated by a desire to 'direct people's attention accurately to the beauty of God's work in the material universe'. It may be worth quoting here in full a passage in which Ruskin demonstrated exactly what, at a concrete level, this strange-sounding ambition might involve: 'Let two persons go out for a walk; the one a good sketcher, the other having no taste of the kind. Let them go down a green lane. There will be a great difference in the scene as perceived by the two individuals. The one will see a lane and trees; he will perceive the trees to be green, though he will think nothing about it; he will see that the sun shines, and that it has a cheerful effect; and that's all! But what will the sketcher see? His eye is accustomed to search into the cause of beauty, and penetrate the minutest parts of loveliness. He looks up, and observes how the showery and subdivided sunshine comes sprinkled down among the gleaming leaves overhead, till the air is filled with the emerald light. He will see here and there a bough emerging from the veil of leaves, he will see the jewel brightness of the emerald moss and the variegated and fantastic lichens, white and blue, purple and red, all mellowed and mingled into a single garment of beauty. Then come the cavernous trunks and the twisted roots that grasp with their snake-like coils at the steep bank,

John Ruskin, *Alpine Peaks,* 1846

whose turfy slope is inlaid with flowers of a thousand dyes. Is not this worth seeing? Yet if you are not a sketcher you will pass along the green lane, and when you come home again, have nothing to say or to think about it, but that you went down such and such a lane.'

7.

Not only did Ruskin encourage us to draw during our travels; he also felt we should write, or 'word-paint', as he called it, so as to cement our impressions of beauty. However respected he was in his lifetime for his drawings, it was his word-paintings that captured the public's imagination and were responsible for his fame in the late Victorian period.

Attractive places typically render us aware of our inadequacies in the area of language. In the Lake District, for example, writing a postcard to a friend, I explained—in some despair and haste—that the scenery was pretty and the weather wet and windy. Ruskin would have ascribed such prose more to laziness than to incapacity. We are all, he argued, able to turn out adequate word paintings; our failure to do so is the result merely of our not asking ourselves enough questions and not being precise enough in analysing what we have seen and felt. Rather than rest with the idea that a lake is pretty, we must ask ourselves more vigorously, 'What in particular is attractive about this stretch of water? What are its associations? What might be a better word for it than *big*?' The finished product may not be marked by genius, but at least it will have been motivated by a search for an authentic representation of an experience.

Ruskin was throughout his adult life frustrated by the refusal of polite, educated English people to talk in sufficient depth about the weather—and in particular by their tendency to refer to it as wet and windy: 'It is a strange thing how little people know about the sky. We never attend to it, we never make it a subject of thought, we look upon it only as a succession of meaningless and monotonous accidents, too common and too vain to be worthy of a moment of watchfulness or a glance of admiration. If in our moments of utter idleness and insipidity, we turn to the sky as a last resource, which of its phenomena do we speak of? One says it has been wet, and another, it has been windy, and another, it has been warm. Who, among the whole chattering crowd, can tell me of the forms and the precipices of the chain of tall white mountains that girded the horizon at noon today? Who saw the narrow sunbeam that came out of the south, and smote upon their summits until they melted and mouldered away in a dust of blue rain? Who saw the dance of the dead clouds when the sunlight left them last night, and the west wind blew them before it like withered leaves?'

The answer was, of course, Ruskin himself, who liked to boast, in another analogy between the function of art and that of eating and drinking, that he bottled skies as carefully as his sherry-importing father did sherries. Here are two diary entries for sky-bottling days in London in the autumn of 1857:

1 November: A vermilion morning, all waves of soft scarlet, sharp at the edge, and gradated to purple. Grey scud moving slowly beneath it from the south-west, heaps of grey cumuli—between the scud and cirrus—at horizon. It issued in an exquisite day.... All purple and blue in distance, and misty sunshine near on the trees, and green fields.... Note the exquisite effect of the golden leaves scattered on the blue sky, and the horse-chestnut, thin and small, dark against them in stars.

3 November: Dawn purple, flushed, delicate. Bank of grey cloud, heavy at six. Then the lighted purple cloud showing through it, open sky of dull yellow above—all grey, and darker scud going across it obliquely, from the south-west—moving fast, yet never stirring from its place, at last melting away. It expands into a sky of brassy flaked light on grey—passes away into grey morning.

8.

The effectiveness of Ruskin's word-painting derived from his method of not only describing what places looked like ('the grass was green, the earth was grey-brown') but also analysing their effect on us in psychological language ('the grass seemed *expansive*, the earth *timid*'). He recognised that many places strike us as beautiful not on the basis of aesthetic criteria—because the colours match or symmetry and proportion are present—but on the basis of psychological criteria, inasmuch as they embody a value or mood of importance to us.

One morning in London, he watched some cumulus clouds from his window. A factual description might have noted that they formed a wall, almost completely white, with a few indentations that allowed some sun through. But Ruskin approached his subject more psychologically: 'The true cumulus, the most majestic of clouds ... is for the most part windless; the movements of its masses being *solemn,* continuous, *inexplicable,* a steady advance or retiring, as if they were *animated* by an *inner will,* or compelled by an unseen power' (emphasis added).

In the Alps, he described pine trees and rocks in similarly psychological terms: 'I can never stay long without awe under an Alpine cliff, looking up to its pines, as they stand on the inaccessible juts and perilous ledges of an enormous wall, in quiet multitudes, each like the shadow of the one beside it—upright, fixed, *not knowing each other.* You cannot reach them, cannot cry to them;—those trees never

Clouds, engraving by J. C. Armytage after a drawing by J. M. W. Turner, from John Ruskin's *Modern Painters*, Vol. 5, 1860

heard human voice; they are far above all sound but of the winds. No foot ever stirred fallen leaf of theirs. All *comfortless* they stand, yet with such *iron will* that the rock itself looks bent and shattered beside them—*fragile, weak, inconsistent*, compared to their dark energy of *delicate life* and *monotony of enchanted pride.'* [*Emphasis added*]

Through such psychological descriptions, we seem to come closer to answering the question of why a place has stirred us. We come closer to the Ruskinian goal of consciously understanding what we have loved.

9.

It would scarcely have been possible to guess that the man parked at the kerb opposite a row of large office blocks was doing some word-painting. The only hint was a notepad pressed against the wheel, on which he occasionally scribbled something between long periods of staring.

It was eleven-thirty at night, and I had been driving around the docks for several hours, stopping for coffee at London City Airport (where I had longingly watched the last flight, a Crossair Avro RJ85, take to the skies, bound for Zurich—or for Baudelaire's 'anywhere! anywhere!'). On my way home, I came upon the giant illuminated towers of the West India Dock. The offices seemed to have no connection with the surrounding landscape of modest and weakly lit houses; they would have been more at home, I thought, on the banks of the Hudson or to one side of the space shuttle at Cape Canaveral. Steam was rising from the top of two adjacent towers, and the whole area had been painted with an even, sparse coating of fog. The lights were still on in most floors, and even from a distance, one could see computer terminals, meeting rooms, potted plants and flipcharts inside.

It was a beautiful scene, and along with the impression of beauty came the desire to possess its source—a desire that, to follow Ruskin, only art could properly satisfy.

I began word-painting. Descriptive passages came most readily: the offices were tall; the top of one tower was like a pyramid; it had ruby-red lights on its side; the sky was not black but an orangey-yellow. But because such a factual description seemed of little help to me in pinning down why I found the scene so impressive, I attempted to analyse its beauty in more psychological terms. The power of the scene appeared to be located in the effect of the night and of the fog on the towers. Night drew attention to facets of the offices that were submerged in the day. Lit by the sun, the offices could seem normal, repelling questions as effectively as their windows repelled glances. But night upset this claim to normality, it allowed one to see inside and wonder at how strange, frightening and admirable they were. The offices embodied order and cooperation among thousands, and at the same time regimentation and tedium. A bureaucratic vision of seriousness was undermined, or at least questioned, by the night. One wondered in the darkness what the flipcharts and office terminals were for: not that they were redundant, just that they might be stranger and more dubitable than daylight had allowed us to think.

At the same time, fog ushered in nostalgia. Foggy nights may, like certain smells, carry us back to other times we experienced them. I thought of nights at university, walking home along illuminated playing fields, and of the differences between my life then and my life now, which led to a bittersweet sadness about the difficulties that had beset me then and the precious things that had since been lost to me.

There were bits of paper all over the car now. The standard of the word-painting was not far above that of my childlike drawing of an oak tree in the Langdale Valley. But quality was not the point. I had at least attempted to follow one strand of what Ruskin judged to be the twin purposes of art: to make sense of pain and to fathom the sources of beauty.

And, as he had pointed out when presented with a series of mis-shapen drawings that a group of his pupils had produced on their travels through the English countryside: 'I believe that the sight is a more important thing than the drawing; and I would rather teach drawing that my pupils may learn to love nature, than teach the looking at nature that they may learn to draw.'

RETURN

IX

On Habit

Place	*Hammersmith, London*
Guide	*Xavier de Maistre*

1.

I returned to London from Barbados to find that the city had stubbornly refused to change. I had seen azure skies and giant sea anemones, I had slept in a raffia bungalow and eaten a kingfish, I had swum beside baby turtles and read in the shade of coconut trees. But my hometown was unimpressed. It was still raining. The park was still a pond; the skies were still funereal. When we are in a good mood and it is sunny, we may be tempted to impute a connection between what happens inside and outside of us, but the appearance of London on my return was a reminder of the indifference of the world to any of the events unfolding in the lives of its inhabitants. I felt despair at being home. I felt there could be few worse places on Earth than the one I had been fated to spend my existence in.

2.

'The sole cause of man's unhappiness is that he does not know how to stay quietly in his room'—Pascal, *Pensées,* 136.

3.

From 1799 to 1804, Alexander von Humboldt undertook a journey around South America, later entitling the account of what he had seen *Journey to the Equinoctial Regions of the New Continent.*

Nine years before Humboldt set out, in the spring of 1790, a twenty-seven-year-old Frenchman named Xavier de Maistre had undertaken a journey around his bedroom, an account of which he would later entitle *Journey around My Bedroom.* Gratified by his experiences, de Maistre in 1798 embarked upon a second journey. This time he travelled by night and ventured out as far as the window ledge; the literary result would be titled *Nocturnal Expedition around My Bedroom*.

Two approaches to travel: *Journey to the Equinoctial Regions of the New Continent; Journey around my Bedroom*. The first required ten mules, thirty pieces of luggage, four interpreters, a chronometer, a sextant, two telescopes, a Borda theodolite, a barometer, a compass, a hygrometer, letters of introduction from the king of Spain and a gun; the latter, a pair of pink-and-blue cotton pyjamas.

Xavier de Maistre was born in 1763, in the picturesque town of Chambéry, at the foot of the French Alps. He was of an intense, romantic nature and was fond of books, especially by Montaigne, Pascal and Rousseau, and of paintings, above all Dutch and French domestic scenes. At the age of twenty-three, de Maistre became fascinated by aeronautics. Etienne Montgolfier had, three years before, achieved international renown by constructing a balloon that flew for eight minutes above the royal palace at Versailles, bearing as passengers a sheep named Montauciel ('Climb-to-the-sky'), a duck and a rooster. De Maistre and a friend fashioned a pair of giant wings out of paper and wire and planned to fly to America. They did not succeed. Two years later de Maistre secured himself a place in a hot-air balloon and spent a few moments floating above Chambéry before the machine crashed into a pine forest.

Then, in 1790, while he was living in a modest room at the top of an apartment building in Turin, de Maistre pioneered a mode of travel that was to make his name: room travel.

Introducing *Journey around My Bedroom*, Xavier's brother, the political theorist Joseph de Maistre, emphasised that it was not Xavier's intention to cast aspersions on the heroic deeds of the great travellers of the past—namely, 'Magellan, Drake, Anson and Cook'. Magellan had discovered a western route to the Spice Islands around the southern tip of South America, Drake had circumnavigated the globe, Anson had produced accurate sea charts of the Philippines and Cook had confirmed the existence of a southern continent. 'They were no doubt remarkable men,' wrote Joseph. It was just that his brother had discovered a way of travelling that might be infinitely more practical for those neither as brave nor as wealthy as those explorers.

'Millions of people who, until now, have never dared to travel, others who have not been able to travel and still more who have not even thought of travelling will be able to follow my example,' explained Xavier as he prepared for his journey. 'The most indolent beings will no longer have any reason to hesitate before setting off to find pleasures that will cost them neither money nor effort.' He particularly recommended room travel to the poor and to those afraid of storms, robbers and high cliffs.

4.

Unfortunately, de Maistre's own pioneering journey, rather like his flying machine, did not get very far.

The story begins well: de Maistre locks his door and changes into his pink-and-blue pyjamas. With no need of luggage, he travels to the sofa, the largest piece of furniture in the room. His journey having shaken him from his usual lethargy, he looks at it through fresh eyes and rediscovers some of its qualities. He admires the elegance of its feet and remembers the pleasant hours he has spent cradled in its cushions, dreaming of love and advancement in his career. From his sofa, de Maistre spies his bed. Once again, from a traveller's vantage point, he learns to appreciate this complex piece of furniture. He feels grateful for the nights he has spent in it and takes pride in the fact that his sheets almost match his pyjamas. 'I advise any man who can do so to get himself pink and white bedlinen,' he writes, for these are colours to induce calm and pleasant reveries in the fragile sleeper.

But thereafter de Maistre may be accused of losing sight of the overall purpose of his endeavour. He becomes mired in long and wearing digressions about his dog, Rosinne, his sweetheart, Jenny, and his faithful servant, Joannetti. Prospective travellers in search of specific guidance on room travel risk coming away from reading *Journey around My Bedroom* feeling a little betrayed.

And yet de Maistre's work sprang from a profound and suggestive insight: the notion that the pleasure we derive from a journey may be dependent more on the mind-set we travel *with* than on the destination we travel *to*. If only we could apply a travelling mind-set to our own locales, we might find these places becoming no less interesting than, say, the high mountain passes and butterfly-filled jungles of Humboldt's South America.

What, then, is a travelling mind-set? Receptivity might be said to be its chief characteristic. Receptive, we approach new places with humility. We carry with us no rigid ideas about what is or is not interesting. We irritate locals because we stand in traffic islands and narrow streets and admire what they take to be unremarkable small details. We risk getting run over because we are intrigued by the roof of a government building or an inscription on a wall. We find a supermarket or a hairdresser's shop unusually fascinating. We dwell at length on the layout of a menu or the clothes of the presenters on the evening news. We are alive to the layers of history beneath the present and take notes and photographs.

Home, by contrast, finds us more settled in our expectations. We feel assured that we have discovered everything interesting about our neighbourhood, primarily by virtue of our having lived there a long time. It seems inconceivable that there could be anything new to find in a place where we have been living for a decade or more. We have become habituated and therefore blind to it.

De Maistre tried to shake us from our passivity. In his second volume of room travel, *Nocturnal Expedition around My Bedroom,* he went to his window and looked up at the night sky. Its beauty made him feel frustrated that such ordinary scenes were not more generally appreciated: 'How few people are right now taking delight in this sublime spectacle that the sky lays on uselessly for dozing humanity! What would it cost those who are out for a walk or crowding out of the theatre to look up for a moment and admire the brilliant constellations that gleam above their heads?' The reason people were not looking was that they had never done so before. They had fallen into the habit of considering their universe to be boring—and their universe had duly fallen into line with their expectations.

5.

I attempted to travel around my bedroom, but it was so small, with barely enough space for a bed, that I concluded that the de Maistrian message might prove more rewarding if it was applied to the neighbourhood as a whole.

So on a clear March day, at around three in the afternoon, several weeks after my return home from Barbados, I set out on a de Maistrian journey around Hammersmith. It felt peculiar to be outside in the middle of the day with no particular destination in mind. A woman and two small blond children were walking along the main road, which was lined with a variety of shops and restaurants. A double-decker bus had stopped to pick up passengers opposite a park. A giant billboard was advertising gravy. I walked along this road almost every day to reach my Underground station and was

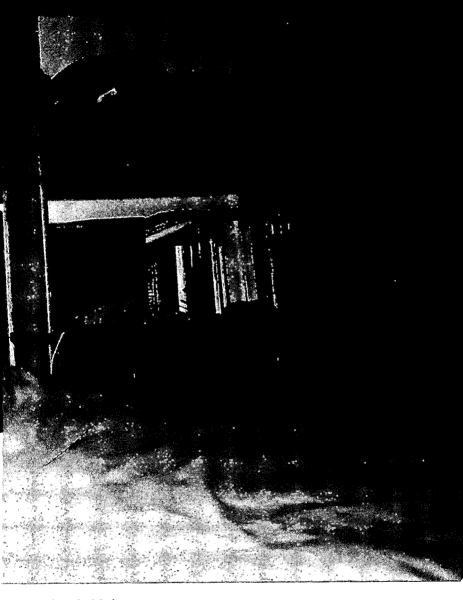

The author's bedroom

unused to regarding it as anything other than a means to my end. Information that assisted me in my goal attracted my attention; all else was judged irrelevant. Thus, while I was sensitive to the number of people on the pavement, as potential impediments to my path, their faces and expressions were invisible to me—as invisible as the shapes of the buildings or the activity in the shops.

It had not always been thus. When I first moved to the area, my attention was less jealously focused. I had at that time not yet settled so firmly on the goal of reaching the Underground quickly.

On entering a new space, our sensitivity is directed towards a number of elements, which we gradually reduce in line with the function we find for the space. Of the four thousand things there might be to see and reflect on in a street, we end up being actively aware of only a few: the number of humans in our path, perhaps, the amount of traffic and the likelihood of rain. A bus that we might at first have viewed aesthetically or mechanically—or even used as a springboard to thoughts about communities within cities—becomes simply a box to move us as rapidly as possible across an area that might as well not exist, so unconnected is it to our primary goal, outside of which all is darkness, all is invisible.

I had imposed a grid of interests on the street, one that left no space for blond children and gravy adverts and paving stones and the colours of shop fronts and the expressions of businesspeople and pensioners. The power of my primary goal had drained me of the will to reflect on the layout of the park or the unusual mixture of Georgian, Victorian and Edwardian architecture along a single block. My walks along the street had been excised of any attentiveness to beauty, any associative thoughts, any sense of wonder or gratitude, any philosophical digressions sparked by visual elements.

In their place, there was simply an insistent call to reach the Underground posthaste.

Now, following de Maistre, I tried to reverse the process of habituation, to dissociate my surroundings from the uses I had previously found for them. I forced myself to obey a strange sort of mental command: I was to look around me as though I had never been in this place before. And slowly, my travels began to bear fruit.

Once I began to consider everything as being of potential interest, objects released latent layers of value. A row of shops that I had always known as one large, undifferentiated, reddish block acquired an architectural identity. There were Georgian pillars around one flower shop, and late-Victorian Gothic-style gargoyles on top of the butcher's. A restaurant became filled with diners rather than shapes. In a glass-fronted office block, people were gesticulating in a boardroom on the first floor as someone drew a pie chart on an overhead projector. Just across the road from the office, a man was pouring out new slabs of concrete for the pavement and carefully shaping their edges. I boarded a bus and, instead of slipping at once into private concerns, tried to connect imaginatively with other passengers. I could hear a conversation in the row ahead of me. Someone in an office somewhere—a person quite high up in the hierarchy, apparently—didn't understand: he complained about how inefficient others were but never reflected on what he himself might be doing to contribute to that inefficiency. I thought of the multiplicity of lives going on at the same time at different levels in a city. I thought of the similarities of complaints—always selfishness, always blindness—and the old psychological truth that what we complain of in others, others will complain of in us.

The neighbourhood did not just acquire people and defined

buildings through my reawakened attention; it also began to collect ideas. I reflected on the new wealth that was spreading into the area. I tried to think why I liked railway arches so much, and why the motorway that cut across the skyline.

It seemed an advantage to be travelling alone. Our responses to the world are crucially moulded by the company we keep, for we temper our curiosity to fit in with the expectations of others. They may have particular visions of who we are and hence may subtly prevent certain sides of us from emerging: 'I hadn't thought of you as someone who was interested in flyovers,' they may intimidatingly suggest. Being closely observed by a companion can also inhibit our observation of others; then, too, we may become caught up in adjusting ourselves to the companion's questions and remarks, or feel the need to make ourselves seem more normal than is good for our curiosity. But alone in Hammersmith in the middle of a March afternoon, I had no such concerns. I had the freedom to act a little weirdly. I sketched the window of a hardware shop and word-painted the flyover.

6.

De Maistre was not only a room traveller. He was also a great traveller in the classic sense. He journeyed to Italy and Russia, spent a winter with the royalist armies in the Alps and fought a Russian campaign in the Caucasus.

In an autobiographical note written in 1801 in South America, Alexander von Humboldt specified his motive for travelling: 'I was spurred on by an uncertain longing to be transported from a boring daily life to a marvellous world.' It was this very dichotomy, 'boring daily life' pitted against 'marvellous world', that de Maistre had tried to redraw with greater subtlety. He would not have suggested to

Humboldt that South America was dull; he merely would have urged him to consider that his native Berlin might have something to offer, too.

Eight decades later, Nietzsche, who had read and admired de Maistre (and spent much time in his own room), picked up on the thought:

When we observe how some people know how to manage their experiences—their insignificant, everyday experiences—so that they become an arable soil that bears fruit three times a year, while others—and how many there are!—are driven through surging waves of destiny, the most multifarious currents of the times and the nations, and yet always remain on top, bobbing like a cork, then we are in the end tempted to divide mankind into a minority (a minimality) of those who know how to make much of little, and a majority of those who know how to make little of much.

There are some who have crossed deserts, floated on ice caps and cut their way through jungles but whose souls we would search in vain for evidence of what they have witnessed. Dressed in pink-and-blue pyjamas, satisfied within the confines of his own bedroom, Xavier de Maistre was gently nudging us to try, before taking off for distant hemispheres, to notice what we have already seen.

Acknowledgements

Thanks to Simon Prosser, Michele Hutchison, Caroline Dawnay, Miriam Gross, Noga Arikha, Nicole Aragi, Dan Frank and Oliver Klimpel.

Picture Acknowledgements

pp. 3, 237 Hammersmith Broadway from *London A–Z Street Atlas* (Reproduced by permission of Geographers' A–Z Map Co. Ltd. Licence No. B1299. This product includes mapping data licensed from Ordnance Survey®. © Crown Copyright 2001. Licence number 100017302)

pp. 3, 209 A Barbados beach (© Bob Krist/CORBIS)

p. 3 Portrait of Joris-Karl Huysmans (detail), photograph by Dornac (*fl.* 1890–1900) (Archives Larousse, Paris/Bridgeman Art Library)

p. 6 *Tahiti Revisited*, 1776, oil on canvas, by William Hodges (© National Maritime Museum, London)

p. 16 *View of Alkmaar, c.* 1670–75, oil on canvas, 44.4 × 43.4 cm, by Jacob Isaacksz van Ruisdael, Dutch (1628/9–82) (Ernest Wadsworth Longfellow Fund, 39.794. Courtesy Museum of Fine Arts, Boston. Reproduced with permission. © 2000. Museum of Fine Arts, Boston. All Rights Reserved)

p. 27 Charles Baudelaire, *c.* 1860, photograph (© Hulton-Deutsch Collection/CORBIS)

p. 27 Edward Hopper, *c.* 1940, photograph by Oscar White (© Oscar White/CORBIS)

p. 50 *Automat,* 1927, oil on canvas, by Edward Hopper (© Francis G. Mayer/CORBIS)

p. 53 *Gas,* 1940, oil on canvas, 66.7 × 102.2 cm, by Edward Hopper (The Museum of Modern Art, New York. Mrs Simon Guggenheim Fund. Photograph © 2001 The Museum of Modern Art, New York)

p. 55 *Compartment C, Car 293,* 1938, oil on canvas, by Edward Hopper (© Geoffrey Clements/CORBIS)

p. 60 *Hotel Room,* 1931, oil on canvas, by Edward Hopper (© Museo Thyssen-Bornemisza, Madrid)

p. 65 Gustave Flaubert, photograph (© Bettmann/CORBIS)

p. 71 *Doors and Bay-Windows in an Arab House* (detail), 1832, watercolour and pencil drawing, by Eugène Delacroix (Département des arts graphiques, Louvre/Photo: © RMN — Gérard Blot)

p. 82 *Bazaar of the Silk Mercers, Cairo,* lithograph by Louis Haghe after a drawing by David Roberts, from *Egypt and Nubia,* published by F. G. Moon, 1849, London (By permission of the British Library)

p. 84 *Private Houses in Cairo,* engraving from Edward William Lane's *An Account of the Manners and Customs of the Modern Egyptians,* 1842, London

p. 89 *Women of Algiers in Their Apartment,* 1834, oil on canvas, by Eugène Delacroix (Louvre, Paris/Photo: © RMN—Arnaudet; J. Schormans)

p. 93 Gustave Flaubert in Cairo, 1850, photograph by Maxime Du Camp (Photo: © RMN—B. Hatala)

p. 99, 104 *Alexander von Humboldt and Aimé Bonpland in Venezuela, c. 1850,* oil on canvas, by Eduard Ender (1822–83) (Brandenburgische Akademie der Wissenschaften, Berlin/AKG London)

p. 113 *Esmeralda, on the Orinoco,* from *Views in the Interior of Guiana,* engraved by Paul Gauci (*fl.* 1834–67), lithograph after a drawing by Charles Bentley (1806–54) (Stapleton Collection/Bridgeman Art Library)

p. 115 *Alexander von Humboldt and Aimé Bonpland at the Foot of Chimborazo,* 1810, oil on canvas, by Friedrich Georg Weitsch (Staatliche Schlösser und Gärten/AKG London)

p. 118 *Géographie des Plantes Equinoxiales,* from *Tableau physique des Andes et Pays voisins,* 1799–1803, by Alexander von Humboldt and Aimé Bonpland (© Royal Geographical Society)

p. 127 *William Wordsworth* (detail), 1842, oil on canvas, by Benjamin Robert Haydon (By courtesy of the National Portrait Gallery, London)

p. 140 *The River Wye at Tintern Abbey,* 1805, oil on canvas, by Philip James de Loutherbourg (1740–1812) (Fitzwilliam Museum, University of Cambridge Bridgeman Art Library)

p. 149 *Kindred Spirits,* 1849, oil on canvas, by Asher Brown Durand (Collections of the New York Public Library, Astor, Lenox and Tilden Foundations)

p. 155 Map of Egypt (detail), from Arthur Penrhyn Stanley's *Sinai and Palestine,* published by John Murray, 1859, London

p. 155 *Edmund Burke* (detail), 1771, oil on canvas, by Sir Joshua Reynolds (By courtesy of the National Portrait Gallery, London)

p. 155 *Job* (detail), oil on canvas, by Léon Joseph Florentin Bonnat (1833–1922) (Musée Bonnat, Bayonne/Lauros/Bridgeman Art Library)

p. 158 *Rocky Mountains, Landers Peak,* 1863, oil on linen, by Albert Bierstadt (Courtesy of the Fogg Art Museum, Harvard University Art Museum, Mrs William Hayes Fogg. Photographic Services © 2001 President and Fellows of Harvard College)

p. 160 *An Avalanche in the Alps,* 1803, oil on canvas, by Philip James de Loutherbourg (Tate, London. © Tate, London 2001)

p. 162 *Chalk Cliffs on Rügen, c.* 1818, oil on canvas, by Caspar David Friedrich (Oskar Reinhart Collection, Winterthur/AKG London)

pp. 179, 190 *Cypresses,* 1889, pencil, quill and reed pen, brown and black ink on wove paper, 62.2 × 47.1 cm, by Vincent van Gogh (Brooklyn Museum of Art, Frank L. Babbott and A. Augustus Healy Funds. © 2001 Brooklyn Museum of Art, New York)

p. 179 *Self-portrait* (detail), 1886/7, oil on artist's board mounted on cradled panel, 41 × 32.5 cm, by Vincent van Gogh, Dutch (1853–90) (Joseph Winterbotham Collection, 1954.326 The Art Institute of Chicago. Photograph © 2001, The Art Institute of Chicago. All rights reserved)

p. 191 *Wheat Field with Cypresses* (detail), 1889, black crayon, pen, reed pen and brown ink on paper, 47 × 62.5 cm, by Vincent van Gogh (Van Gogh Museum, Amsterdam/Vincent van Gogh Foundation)

p. 195 *Olive Grove: Orange Sky,* 1889, oil on canvas, by Vincent van Gogh (Collection Rijksmuseum Kröller-Müller, Otterlo)

p. 198 *'The Yellow House' (Vincent's House), Arles,* 1888, oil on canvas, by Vincent van Gogh (Rijksmuseum Vincent van Gogh, Amsterdam/AKG London)

p. 208 *Sunset: Wheat Fields near Arles,* 1888, oil on canvas, by Vincent van Gogh (Kunstmuseum Winterthur, Winterthur. © 2001)

p. 211 West India Docks from *London A–Z Street Atlas* (Reproduced by permission of Geographers' A–Z Map Co. Ltd. Licence No. B1299.

This product includes mapping data licensed from Ordnance Survey®. © Crown Copyright 2001. Licence number 100017302)

p. 211 *John Ruskin* (detail), 1879, watercolour, by Sir Hubert von Herkomer (Courtesy of the National Portrait Gallery, London)

p. 221 *Study of a Peacock's Breast Feather,* 1873, watercolour, by John Ruskin (Collection of the Guild of St George, Sheffield Galleries & Museums Trust)

p. 223 *Velvet Crab, c.* 1870–71, pencil, watercolour and bodycolour, on grey-blue paper, by John Ruskin (Ashmolean Museum, Oxford/Bridgeman Art Library)

p. 224 *Branches,* drawing by John Ruskin from John Ruskin's *Elements of Drawing,* 1857, London

p. 226 *Alpine Peaks,* 1846, pencil, watercolour and bodycolour, on three joined sheets, by John Ruskin (Birmingham Museums and Art Gallery)

p. 230 *Clouds,* engraving by J. C. Armytage after a drawing by J. M. W. Turner, from John Ruskin's *Modern Painters,* Vol. 5, 1860, London

p. 237 *Le Comte Xavier de Maistre (1764–1852)* (detail), engraving by Baron de Steuben (Photo: © Roger-Viollet)

All other photographs were taken by the author.

About the Author

Alain de Botton is the author of *On Love, The Romantic Movement, Kiss and Tell, How Proust Can Change Your Life,* and *The Consolations of Philosophy.* His work has been translated into twenty languages. He lives in Washington, D.C., and London. He can be reached at *www.alaindebotton.com*